Teenage Eating Disorders

Teenage Problems

ReferencePoint
Press®

San Diego, CA

Other books in the Compact Research Teenage Problems set:

Teenage Alcoholism
Teenage Drug Abuse
Teenage Mental Illness
Teenage Sex and Pregnancy
Teenage Suicide

*For a complete list of titles please visit www.referencepointpress.com.

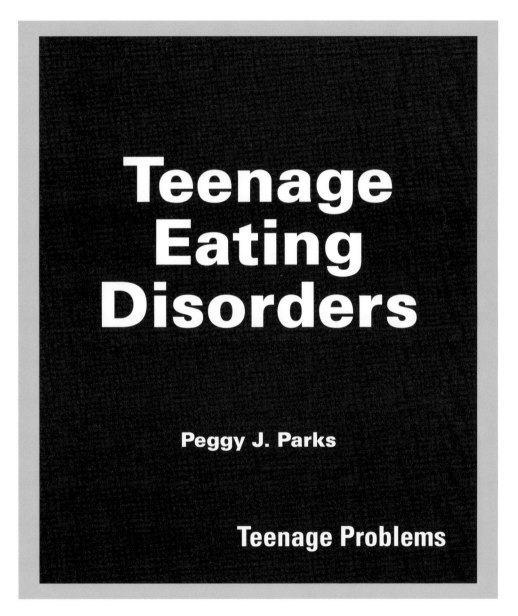

Teenage
Eating
Disorders

Peggy J. Parks

Teenage Problems

ReferencePoint
Press®

San Diego, CA

For more information, contact:
ReferencePoint Press, Inc.
PO Box 27779
San Diego, CA 92198
www.ReferencePointPress.com

Picture credits:
Cover: iStockphoto.com and Thinkstock/Comstock
Maury Aaseng: 33–34, 47–48, 61–62, 75–77
AP Images: 13, 20

LIBRARY OF CONGRESS CATALOGING-IN-PUBLICATION DATA

Parks, Peggy J., 1951–
    Teenage eating disorders / by Peggy J. Parks.
        p. cm. — (Compact research series)
    Includes bibliographical references and index.
    ISBN-13: 978-1-60152-166-8 (hardback)
    ISBN-10: 1-60152-166-9 (hardback)
    1. Eating disorders in adolescence—Juvenile literature. I. Title.
    RJ506.E18P37   2012
    616.85'2600835—dc22
                                                                    2011001383

Contents

Foreword

❝Where is the knowledge we have lost in information?❞

—T.S. Eliot, "The Rock."

As modern civilization continues to evolve, its ability to create, store, distribute, and access information expands exponentially. The explosion of information from all media continues to increase at a phenomenal rate. By 2020 some experts predict the worldwide information base will double every 73 days. While access to diverse sources of information and perspectives is paramount to any democratic society, information alone cannot help people gain knowledge and understanding. Information must be organized and presented clearly and succinctly in order to be understood. The challenge in the digital age becomes not the creation of information, but how best to sort, organize, enhance, and present information.

ReferencePoint Press developed the *Compact Research* series with this challenge of the information age in mind. More than any other subject area today, researching current issues can yield vast, diverse, and unqualified information that can be intimidating and overwhelming for even the most advanced and motivated researcher. The *Compact Research* series offers a compact, relevant, intelligent, and conveniently organized collection of information covering a variety of current topics ranging from illegal immigration and deforestation to diseases such as anorexia and meningitis.

The series focuses on three types of information: objective single-author narratives, opinion-based primary source quotations, and facts and statistics. The clearly written objective narratives provide context and reliable background information. Primary source quotes are carefully selected and cited, exposing the reader to differing points of view. And facts and statistics sections aid the reader in evaluating perspectives. Presenting these key types of information creates a richer, more balanced learning experience.

For better understanding and convenience, the series enhances information by organizing it into narrower topics and adding design features that make it easy for a reader to identify desired content. For example, in *Compact Research: Illegal Immigration*, a chapter covering the economic impact of illegal immigration has an objective narrative explaining the various ways the economy is impacted, a balanced section of numerous primary source quotes on the topic, followed by facts and full-color illustrations to encourage evaluation of contrasting perspectives.

The ancient Roman philosopher Lucius Annaeus Seneca wrote, "It is quality rather than quantity that matters." More than just a collection of content, the *Compact Research* series is simply committed to creating, finding, organizing, and presenting the most relevant and appropriate amount of information on a current topic in a user-friendly style that invites, intrigues, and fosters understanding.

Teenage Eating Disorders at a Glance

Eating Disorders Defined

Eating disorders are mental illnesses that involve an obsession with food, extremely unhealthy eating behaviors, and a distorted body image.

Types

The two most common eating disorders are anorexia and bulimia. A third category, called "eating disorder not otherwise specified," includes binge-eating disorder.

Prevalence

Experts estimate that up to 1 percent of the US population suffers from anorexia, and up to 3 percent from bulimia, with the majority of cases being adolescent females. Binge-eating disorder is the most common eating disorder, but not among teenagers.

Warning Signs

Initial symptoms of anorexia include an obsession with food and dieting, weight loss, dizziness and fainting, and a pale, sickly appearance. Bulimia sufferers eat massive amounts of food and then disappear immediately after a meal in order to force themselves to vomit.

Causes

Scientists believe that eating disorders result from a complex interaction of genetic, cultural, and psychological factors.

Health Risks

Both anorexia and bulimia can cause low blood pressure, deficiencies of essential minerals known as electrolytes, and severe damage to vital organs such as the kidneys, liver, and heart. Of all the mental illnesses, these eating disorders collectively have the highest fatality rate.

Prevention

Experts say programs that focus on the dangers of eating disorders could potentially keep teens from developing them, but such programs are much rarer than those that focus on drug and alcohol awareness.

Overcoming Eating Disorders

Treatment programs have been shown to help many teens recover from eating disorders, but the National Association of Anorexia Nervosa and Associated Disorders states that only 1 in 10 sufferers receive treatment.

Overview

Overview

❝Eating disorders are real, complex, and devastating conditions that can have serious consequences for health, productivity, and relationships. They are not a fad, phase or lifestyle choice.❞

> —The National Eating Disorders Association, which serves as a resource for prevention, cures, and access to quality care for people affected by eating disorders and their families.

❝Eating disorders can virtually take over your life. You may think about food all the time, spend hours agonizing over what to eat, and exercise to exhaustion. You may feel ashamed, sad, hopeless, drained, irritable and anxious.❞

> —Mayo Clinic, a world-renowned medical facility headquartered in Rochester, Minnesota.

Krista Phelps was known for many different qualities, including her passion for giving 100 percent to anything she undertook. At her high school in Kingsley, Iowa, she was a straight-A student, a cheerleader, and a member of the volleyball and track teams. She especially loved track. Her father had been a national champion discus thrower, and she was on the way toward following in his footsteps. As a sophomore Phelps was ranked fifteenth in the state for discus, and at the May 21, 2010, state finals in Des Moines, she took sixth place. She was pleased with that ranking, as she wrote in a text message: "I was ranked 15th I got sixth, and the first five places were juniors and seniors, so I'm satisfied."[1]

Two days after the competition, on a muggy Sunday morning, Phelps went for her usual jog. When she did not return home, her mother became concerned and went looking for her—and found her lying on the side of the road. Phelps had died at the age of 16, her life cut short by complications from the eating disorder anorexia nervosa, which she had battled for nearly a year. "It's a bad thing, this disease," says her coach, Randy Wiese. "I don't think anybody realized the severity of it, including me. I had no idea."[2]

What Are Eating Disorders?

If eating disorders could be summed up in one word, it would be *extreme*. They are complicated, serious mental disorders that affect people of all ages but typically strike during adolescence. The National Institute of Mental Health says that someone with an eating disorder "experiences severe disturbances in eating behavior, such as extreme reduction of food intake or extreme overeating, or feelings of extreme distress or concern about body weight or shape."[3] The eating disorders that are officially recognized as mental illnesses by the American Psychiatric Association are anorexia nervosa, bulimia nervosa, and a category of problem eating behaviors officially called "eating disorder not otherwise specified." Binge-eating disorder falls under the latter category.

Anorexia is characterized by an obsessive pursuit of thinness that the sufferer tries to accomplish through self-starvation. Mayo Clinic psychiatrist Alexander R. Lucas describes someone in the grip of anorexia: "Such women become emaciated hollow shells with cadaver-like faces, their sallow skin drawn tightly over their fragile bones."[4] Those who have bulimia (from the Greek words meaning *ox hunger*) regularly eat enormous amounts of food and then purge to get rid of it, which mental health professionals call the binge-purge cycle. Most bulimics do this by forcing themselves to vomit, but they may also regularly take laxatives to empty the bowels and/or use diuretics (water pills) to remove fluids from the body.

> " **The National Institute of Mental Health states that the one eating disorder that roughly affects males and females equally is binge-eating disorder.** "

Binge-eating disorder is similar to bulimia in that sufferers have bouts of gorging on food, often high-calorie meals and sweets, to the point of discomfort and physical pain. Unlike bulimia, however, those with binge-eating disorder do not vomit after eating or use other methods to purge their bodies of food. They tend to be overweight, often obese, because they regularly consume far more calories than their body can use or burn off.

Millions of Sufferers

Health experts estimate that up to 1 percent of the US population suffers from anorexia and from 1 to 3 percent suffers from bulimia. These eating disorders can affect people of all ages, but both develop during adolescence far more often than later in life. These numbers are based on tallies of people who have sought treatment, and most do not. But even though prevalence data may not be exact, it *is* accurate to say that millions of teenagers suffer from eating disorders.

> **Over time, anorexia causes skin to have a sickly pallor, as well as dizziness and fainting, and in females the cessation of menstruation, a condition known as amenorrhea.**

According to the National Institute of Mental Health, females are 3 times more likely to suffer from anorexia and/or bulimia than males. But again, this is based on cases that have been reported. Since females seek professional help far more often than males, the actual number of male sufferers is undoubtedly higher than is projected. Child and adolescent psychologist Mae Sokol explains: "The public thinks of it as a 'girl disease,' and these guys don't want to have to come out and say, 'I have a girl disease.' Plus, to have to come to a [treatment facility] where most of the patients are women— they don't feel good about that at all."[5]

The National Institute of Mental Health states that the one eating disorder that roughly affects males and females equally is binge-eating disorder. It is the most common of all eating disorders, although this is not true for teenagers. Young people do develop binge-eating disorder, but most sufferers are middle-aged to older adults.

At age 21, this young woman illustrates the toll and the challenges of anorexia: A former university swimmer, she stands 5 feet, 4 inches tall and weighs just 75 pounds. She underwent treatment but then relapsed, explaining that negative thinking often overpowers rational thought.

From No Eating to Gluttonous Eating

The eating habits of people who suffer from eating disorders are appallingly unhealthy. Those with anorexia, for instance, often subsist on starvation diets that may include nothing more than tomatoes and apples, or several meals a day consisting only of grapes. The National Eating Disorders Association says that some anorexia sufferers "may eat candy bars in the morning and nothing else all day. Others may eat lettuce and mustard every 2 hours or only condiments."[6]

The diets of teens with bulimia or binge-eating disorder are radically different; rather than starving themselves, they eat massive amounts of food. In referring to someone with bulimia, Chicago psychiatrist Kimberly Dennis writes: "Food can be consumed so fast that sometimes it's not even chewed or tasted. An average binge can consist of 1,500–3,000 calories, the equivalent of an entire large deep-dish pizza or a full-size birthday cake, although some individuals eat much more during a binge."[7]

Warning Signs

Eating disorders are not always easy for parents and other individuals to spot in someone they care about. The Mayo Clinic writes: "In children it's sometimes hard to tell what's an eating disorder and what's simply a whim, a new fad, or experimentation with a vegetarian diet or other eating styles."[8] In terms of symptoms, anorexia tends to be the most obvious. The first sign is often a sudden, intense fear of gaining weight, followed by strict dieting, avoiding meals, and an obsession with measuring food portions and counting every calorie and fat gram. Another common warning sign is excessive exercise, as the anorexic attempts to burn off the few calories he or she has consumed.

Genetics is an important factor because eating disorders tend to run in families.

As anorexic teens steadily continue to lose weight, they become very thin and frail. They often wear baggy clothing in an effort to disguise their extreme weight loss, as one teenage girl said to her therapist, Anna Bardone-Cone: "I feel like I always have to wear these bulky clothes because if I don't, people will see me and, like, freak out."[9] Over time, anorexia causes skin to have a sickly pallor, as well as dizziness and fainting, and in females the cessation of menstruation, a condition known as amenorrhea. Because malnourishment causes body temperature to drop, anorexia sufferers feel cold all the time and cannot get warm even under thick blankets. The body's way of compensating for this heat loss is to grow its own protective "blanket," a layer of soft, downy hair known as lanugo.

Symptoms of bulimia are often less noticeable than anorexia, at least at first, because those who suffer from it tend to be of normal weight, or even slightly overweight. The most obvious symptom is when a person starts eating enormous amounts of food in one sitting, and then disappears immediately afterward, a likely sign that he or she has gone to the bathroom to vomit. Other bulimia symptoms (caused by forced vomiting) include burst blood vessels in the eyes, chronically inflamed and sore throat, and enlarged salivary glands in the cheeks, a condition known as "chipmunk cheeks." Frequent vomiting can also destroy the teeth. When bulimia sufferers vomit repeatedly, highly corrosive gastric acids flood the teeth and destroy their protective enamel covering. Over time, this causes extensive decay and can literally cause teeth to crumble.

Why Do Teenagers Develop Eating Disorders?

Eating disorders are mysterious illnesses for which no definitive cause has been found. Scientists theorize that a complex combination of biology, personality type, and environmental/societal factors work together in the development of eating disorders. Two known risk factors are being female, since girls and young women have a higher risk of developing anorexia or bulimia than males; and age, because adolescents are at greater risk than adults.

Genetics is an important factor because eating disorders tend to run in families. Research has shown that someone with a parent or sibling who has an eating disorder has a significantly higher risk of also developing one. Psychiatrist Kathleen N. Franco writes: "First-degree female relatives and monozygotic [identical] twin offspring of patients with anorexia nervosa have higher rates of anorexia nervosa and bulimia nervosa. Children of patients with anorexia nervosa have a lifetime risk for anorexia nervosa that is tenfold that of the general population."[10]

High-Risk Teens

Although all teens are potentially vulnerable to developing eating disorders, some have a markedly higher risk than others. As Krista Phelps's tragic death shows, many athletes suffer from anorexia and/or bulimia because they often eat diets that are unhealthily low in calories and fat, while pushing themselves extremely hard to succeed. According to the Mayo Clinic, this is especially true of runners, gymnasts, and wrestlers, all of whom are at high risk of falling prey to eating disorders. Also at risk are figure skaters and ballet dancers, who are under constant pressure to remain rail-thin and often suffer from either anorexia or bulimia. The Mayo Clinic adds that coaches and parents may unwittingly contribute to the development of eating disorders among young athletes by encouraging them to lose weight.

> One profession that is notorious for demanding ultra-skinny bodies is modeling, which is why a disproportionately high number of models suffer from eating disorders.

One profession that is notorious for demanding ultra-skinny bodies is modeling, which is why a disproportionately high number of models suffer from eating disorders. One example is Alexandra Michael, who was in the throes of anorexia when she started her modeling career as a teenager. By the time she was 18, Michael had sought treatment and was getting back to a normal size—but at the 2008 Fashion Week in Paris, France, more than one casting director remarked that she was fat. "I used to think of being skinny as a job requirement," she says. "I felt pressure to be emaciated. It's not even just a pressure to be thin. It's a pressure to be skeletal."[11]

Media Glamorization

Research has clearly shown that young people, primarily girls, are influenced by the appearance and behavior of celebrities whom they idolize. When these famous people appear in fashion or entertainment magazines, in movies, or on television looking glamorous—and rail-thin—this can have a profound effect on vulnerable teens. In a futile effort to look like their idols, they may resort to drastic measures such as self-starvation, which could lead to an eating disorder.

This is all too familiar to Rosalind Ponomarenko-Jones, a British woman whose teenage daughter died from anorexia. She decries the media's glamorization of super-skinny celebrities, saying that these emaciated models and actresses have "inordinate influence" over teenagers who idolize them and want to look like them. She writes: "My real fear is that millions of impressionable young women will seek to emulate this new breed of 'twiglet' celebrities. Small wonder that growing numbers of teenagers are falling prey to eating disorders, when role models in magazines exhibit their jutting bones and attenuated limbs while breezily declaring they've barely noticed their dangerously diminishing size."[12]

Yet the blame for eating disorders cannot solely be placed on the media, because the majority of teens do not develop them. Young people all over the world pore over glitzy photos and gaze longingly at ultra-thin celebrities on television and in movies. And while they may feel envious, this does not cause them to starve themselves or begin forcing themselves to vomit. Still, experts say the ubiquitous media publicity can serve as a trigger for impressionable

> " It is common for teens with eating disorders to also suffer from other mental illnesses, which is known as comorbidity. "

teens who are biologically vulnerable. That is what Ponomarenko-Jones is convinced happened to her daughter, as she writes: "I do not believe that the pageant of ghoulishly thin women we see every time we open a magazine will actually be the sole cause of eating disorders in our children. But it will contribute to their illness; I have no doubt about that."[13]

Accompanying Mental Disorders

It is common for teens with eating disorders to also suffer from other mental illnesses, which is known as comorbidity. As the National Eating Disorders Association explains: "Eating disorders are usually related to emotional issues such as control and low self-esteem and often exist as part of a 'dual' diagnosis of major depression, anxiety, or obsessive-compulsive disorder."[14] Franco adds that the most common mental illness associated with eating disorders is depression, with comorbidity being from 50 to 75 percent.

Psychologists have also found a close tie between anorexia and bulimia and self-injury disorder, whereby people cut themselves or intentionally harm their bodies in other ways. Psychologist Sharon Farber, who specializes in eating disorders, researched this in depth and found many commonalities. In reference to similarities between people with bulimia and those who self-injure, Farber explains: "Both of them seemed to be an individual's attempt to solve emotional problems, to make himself or herself feel better. . . . I found that the self-injurious behavior and the bulimic behavior, especially the purging (which is the most painful part of that experience), were being used as an attempt to release tension or to interrupt or end a feeling of depression or extreme anxiety."[15]

What Are the Dangers of Eating Disorders?

Eating disorders can be devastating, causing a number of severe health problems. For instance, the malnutrition caused by anorexia can cause hormonal imbalance, the depletion of crucial minerals, and loss of bone density, which can lead to a serious bone disease known as osteoporosis. Self-starvation also wastes away body fat. For young people who want to be thinner, this may sound appealing—but it can destroy the body's muscle. Lucas describes the inevitable result if all fat has been starved away: "After a considerable amount of body fat is lost, muscle tissue becomes depleted as well, as the body begins to break down muscle cells for energy. This results in ketosis, the accumulation of ketone bodies in the blood, which is a sign of starvation."[16] Once the body begins to consume muscle, this can starve vital organs such as the kidneys, liver, and heart, continuing to weaken them until they eventually fail.

> **Even though the fatality rate for bulimia is not as high as that of anorexia, the disorder can also be deadly.**

Anorexia is the deadliest of all eating disorders. Studies have shown that people who suffer from anorexia are up to 12 times more likely to die compared with those who do not have the disorder. Death can result from major organ failure or from deficiencies in essential minerals in the bloodstream known as electrolytes. Proper electrolyte balance is crucial—without it, the heart can rapidly fail. This is what happened to Krista Phelps. Although she was slowly starting to gain back some of the weight she had lost, a severe electrolyte imbalance ultimately caused her death.

Even though the fatality rate for bulimia is not as high as that of anorexia, the disorder can also be deadly. Forced vomiting can lead to rup-
tures in the esophagus, which is the tube that carries food, liquids, and
saliva from the mouth to the stomach. Other serious health effects include internal bleeding and severe damage to kidneys, bowels, and liver.
Fluid loss from vomiting and use of laxatives and/or diuretics can cause
severe dehydration, thus depleting the body of essential minerals. As with
anorexia, electrolyte imbalances can result in death.

Eating Disorder Prevention

With growing awareness of the severity of eating disorders, advocacy
groups say that prevention programs targeted at young people are crucial.
Programs offered through organizations such as the Girl Scouts of America have been shown to reduce risk factors for eating disorders among
participants. Yet these sorts of programs are sorely lacking throughout
the United States, as the National Association of Anorexia Nervosa and
Associated Disorders explains: "Only a small number of schools and col-
leges have programs to educate our youth about the dangers of eating
disorders." The group stresses that prevention must become a priority:
"The immense suffering surrounding eating disorders, the high cost of
treatment, and the longevity of those illnesses make it imperative that
vastly expanded education programs be implemented to prevent anorexia
nervosa and related disorders."[17]

Psychologist and author Michael Levine also believes that prevention
efforts are important for youth, but he says that some approaches can do
more harm than good. For instance, programs that merely lecture students and treat them "as ignorant and easily led astray by culture" can be
detrimental rather than effective. Levine writes: "These programs run the
risk of being a waste of time, and, worse of being either voyeuristic (e.g.,
'look at the horrible, thin anorexic people') or of inadvertently promoting unhealthy means of weight management. One prominent sign of an
ineffective program is students who are disinterested because they do not
see the issues as having anything to do with them."[18]

Can Teenagers Overcome Eating Disorders?

Overcoming an eating disorder can be challenging for anyone, and this
is especially true for teenagers. Adolescence is a time when young people

Teenagers with eating disorders can overcome their conditions but to do so requires determination and hard work. Counseling provides one important means of recovery from eating disorders. Programs such as Food Addicts Anonymous (pictured) also provide support.

are already struggling with emotional issues. For them to acknowledge that they suffer from an eating disorder and need help can be overwhelming, so they feel unable to face it. As psychiatrist David Schlager explains:

"Like most young people, they pretend it's not happening."[19] Yet Schlager says that even with the challenges involved, if teenagers get treatment, recovery is possible.

Mental health professionals overwhelmingly agree that therapy is essential for treating eating disorders, and many are convinced that it should involve the whole family. James Lock, who is a professor of psychiatry and behavioral sciences at Stanford University's School of Medicine, says that including the family can be beneficial for everyone involved. He explains: "The idea here is that the disorder is disabling and confusing to both the patient and to the family, and that the family actually needs to learn how to help directly solve the problem of the child eating and over-exercising, and find solutions at home where the child is living."[20]

Lingering Mysteries

Whether eating disorders involve self-starvation or binge eating, they are frightening and life-threatening illnesses. Although a number of risk factors have been identified, including genetics, age, gender, and societal influences, a definitive cause is not known. The road to recovery is often difficult and filled with many challenges. But with the right treatment, it is possible for teens to overcome eating disorders and go on to live normal, healthy lives.

What Are Eating Disorders?

> 66Eating disorders involve serious disturbances in eating behavior, such as extreme and unhealthy reduction of food intake or severe overeating, as well as feelings of distress or extreme concern about body shape or weight.99

—Alliance for Eating Disorders Awareness, which seeks to educate the public about the dangers of eating disorders and reduce the rate and severity of these disorders among people of all ages.

> 66Eating disorders are treacherous. They destroy and even take lives, and they make sufferers doubt and hate themselves.99

—Susan Schulherr, a psychotherapist from New York City and the author of *Eating Disorders for Dummies*.

Claudia Faniello was 14 years old when bulimia seized control of her life. A well-known singer from the island country of Malta, Faniello was conscious of her body and convinced herself that the success of her singing career depended on her ability to keep her weight down. "I felt chubby and was unhappy with the way I looked," she says. "I don't remember the moment I realised I could get rid of the food I ate by throwing up." Once she had that realization, Faniello became obsessed with forcing herself to vomit every time she ate: "It was like a monster living inside me, something which stole my identity."[21]

Faniello began to feel like she was in the clutches of a powerful drug addiction. She was aware that what she was doing to herself was harmful, but she felt incapable of stopping it. The burning need to get rid of every single thing she ate or drank dominated her thoughts, from the time she first woke up in the morning until she fell asleep at night. She explains: "My life started revolving around the minutes I spent in the bathroom throwing up and the amazing feeling of victory I felt later. It became addictive, just like a drug."[22] Finally, something happened that opened Faniello's eyes to the damage she was inflicting on her body. She started losing her singing voice because stomach acid from frequent vomiting had damaged her vocal cords.

Internal Demons

The very idea that her ability to sing could be destroyed by her own behavior was terrifying to Faniello. Yet this fear ultimately led to a positive outcome because it motivated her to get help and to eventually overcome bulimia. She explains: "My voice was the only thing I liked about myself and I was afraid of losing it. That was what gave me the courage to stop."[23] Like Faniello, teens who suffer from eating disorders often feel as though an outside force has taken control of their lives. They become so obsessed with weight and body shape that they can focus on little else. They begin to feel like there is no escape from the relentless hold that their eating disorder has on them.

According to New York psychotherapist Susan Schulherr, at the root of eating disorders is the compulsiveness of the symptoms and the sufferers' inner drive to be thin. She explains: "Compulsions are behaviors that have an 'I *have* to' urgency associated with them—to the point that the person often no longer feels they are a matter of voluntary control."[24] Schulherr adds that the self-worth of those with eating disorders becomes totally dependent on how successful they are at dieting and losing weight. Thus, their mood "rises and falls" based on the numbers they see on the scale. She writes: "What probably started out as ordinary dieting has developed into a rigid pattern that has gone seriously out of control. As time goes on, your eating disorder takes up more and more space while the rest of your life—friends, family, fun, future—takes up less and less."[25]

> Teens who suffer from eating disorders often feel as though an outside force has taken control of their lives.

Flawed Perceptions

Anorexia and bulimia have only been recognized as mental illnesses since the 1980s, when the American Psychiatric Association added them to its *Diagnostic and Statistical Manual of Mental Disorders*. In the years since that designation was made, awareness of eating disorders has grown dramatically. Today scientists have a much better understanding of how serious these disorders are and how dangerous they can be for those who suffer from them.

Another change over the past few decades is the repudiation of the belief that only girls from wealthy families suffer from eating disorders. This was once the prevailing theory and was evident in a 1978 book called *The Golden Cage: The Enigma of Anorexia Nervosa* by the late psychiatrist Hilde Bruch. She wrote: "New diseases are rare, and a disease that selectively befalls the young, rich, and beautiful is practically unheard of. But such a disease is affecting the daughters of well-to-do, educated, and successful families. . . . The chief symptom is severe starvation leading to a devastating weight loss; 'she looks like the victim of a concentration camp' is a not uncommon description."[26]

> "One of the most puzzling aspects of eating disorders—and a major factor in why they are so difficult to treat—is that sufferers have a grossly distorted view of their own bodies."

Yet even though knowledge about eating disorders has grown since Bruch's book was published, old misconceptions linger—including among some who work in the mental health field. Despite all that has been learned through the years, eating disorders are still often viewed as an attention-getting condition most common among girls from wealthy families. This is frustrating for professionals who treat patients with eating disorders, as Julie O'Toole, a pediatrician who founded the Kartini Clinic for Disordered Eating, writes: "So, gone are the days when patients suffering from this illness faced guilt and social stigma, blamed for 'choosing' the behaviors that characterize anorexia, right? Well, apparently not quite. While the science is unequivocal, some [health-care] providers' opinions (and practices) are still resistant to change."[27]

Another flawed perception is that eating disorders only affect young, white females. While anorexia and bulimia are most common in this group, studies show that prevalence is growing in males as well as in people of other ethnicities. In short, eating disorders do not discriminate based on race, gender, or socioeconomic status. As the Alliance for Eating Disorders Awareness states, "No one is immune."[28]

Rodolfo Ruiz, who developed anorexia as a teenager, does not fit the typical profile of someone with an eating disorder. During his childhood Ruiz had been teased and called cruel names because he was overweight. Disgusted with himself, he often stared at his image in the mirror and pinched the roll of fat that he could see peeking out from under his shirt. Raised on rich, fattening Mexican cooking, Ruiz had no idea how to eat a healthier diet—so he stopped eating altogether. In a September 2008 *Newsweek* article, journalist Jessica Bennett writes: "As a teen, the once chubby boy became so thin, his vision often blurred. He guzzled gallons of Lipton diet iced tea, and jogged five miles each day, dropping—at 17 years old and 5 feet 6 inches—to 104 pounds."[29]

Seeing Is Believing

One of the most puzzling aspects of eating disorders—and a major factor in why they are so difficult to treat—is that sufferers have a grossly distorted view of their own bodies. As unbelievable as it may seem, a painfully thin person with an eating disorder (most notably anorexia) will stand in front of a mirror and actually see an obese person gazing back. Sacramento State University psychology professor Kim Roberts explains: "Someone with anorexia may be 90 pounds, but when they look in the mirror they see themselves as fat. The longer this person goes without treatment, the more embedded the body-image problem becomes."[30]

This was true of Johanna S. Kandel, who developed anorexia when she was in the seventh grade and battled it for 10 years. Even as the pounds continued to melt off her already-thin body, and worried friends, teachers, and ballet instructors started asking if she was sick, Kandel remained convinced that she was still not skinny enough. She writes: "If you've ever looked in one of those fun-house mirrors that makes you look extremely distorted, you'll know what I saw when I looked at my reflection. The only difference is that when you're in the fun house, it's the mirror that's doing the distorting, but for me it was what my brain thought it saw."[31]

Two Disorders in One

Anorexia and bulimia have very different symptoms, with the former involving self-starvation and the latter involving binge eating and purging. Yet these disorders are more alike than many people realize. In spite of their differences, they are rooted in the same deep psychological problems, as New York psychologist Andrea D. Vazzana explains: "With both disorders, the individual's primary means of self-evaluation is through shape and weight."[32] Because of the common thread between anorexia and bulimia, many teens suffer from both. According to Cleveland Clinic psychiatrist Kathleen N. Franco, up to 50 percent of patients with anorexia develop symptoms of bulimia, while a smaller percentage of bulimics later develop anorexic symptoms.

> As awareness of eating disorders has continued to grow, mental health professionals have become aware of a 'hybrid' disorder that has characteristics of anorexia and bulimia. Known as bulimarexia, it involves self-starvation, followed by bouts of binge eating and purging.

As awareness of eating disorders has continued to grow, mental health professionals have become aware of a "hybrid" disorder that has characteristics of anorexia and bulimia. Known as bulimarexia, it involves self-starvation, followed by bouts of binge eating and purging. Anna Paterson, an author and public speaker who struggled with anorexia for 14 years, writes: "Sufferers have many of the traits of anorexia—they are underweight and consistently restrict their food intake. They may allow themselves to eat certain low-calorie food, such as fruit, vegetables, rice cakes, crispbread and yoghurt. However, even after eating this diet food, the guilt is so intense that sufferers force themselves to vomit in a similar way to bulimia sufferers."[33]

A teenager named Laura Peachey has created a Facebook page for those who suffer from bulimarexia. She says that she is a "victim" of the disorder and describes how it affects someone who has it: "A person who has bulimarexia will bounce back and forth from the symptoms of one condition to the symptoms of the other. She will display some periods of restricting her food intake to nearly none, and some periods of stuffing in large quantities of food, removing it from her body afterward with purging."

> " Although people with orthorexia are not concerned with their weight, they become so fixated on healthy eating that they avoid numerous foods that contain essential nutrients. This can result in dramatic weight loss and severe malnutrition. "

Peachey says that when an anorexia sufferer develops bulimic behaviors, people may assume that he or she is recovering from anorexia, but nothing could be further from the truth. She writes: "Instead, it is a sign that the person is no longer able to even hold to one pattern, and so goes back and forth from one to the other. Not only is this state potentially life threatening, the psychological implications can be equally deadly."[34]

The "Healthy Diet" Eating Disorder

At the heart of eating disorders is an obsession with food and body image, which involves diets that are extraordinarily unhealthy. So the notion that someone who is rigid about eating only healthy foods could actually have an eating disorder seems incongruous—yet it is a reality for those who suffer from orthorexia nervosa. A little-known and somewhat controversial eating disorder, orthorexia is characterized by an obsession with eating only foods that are natural and pure—the quest for the perfect diet. Steven Bratman, a physician from California who originally coined the term *orthorexia*, explains: "I realize this sounds like an oxymoron. How can focusing on healthy food be bad for you? The apparent contradiction has led to a great deal of challenge of the concept. But the emphasis is intended to be on 'unhealthy obsession.'"[35]

Although people with orthorexia are not concerned with their weight, they become so fixated on healthy eating that they avoid numerous foods that contain essential nutrients. This can result in dramatic weight loss and severe malnutrition, as Bratman writes: "Emaciation is common among followers of certain health food diets, such as raw foodism, and this can at times reach the extremes seen in anorexia nervosa. Such 'anorexic orthorexia' is just as dangerous as anorexia." Bratman has personally witnessed the deadly effects of orthorexia because it claimed the life of one of his patients, Kate Finn. "She wasn't afraid of being fat," he says. "She didn't want to be thin. She just wanted to eat healthy food. Nonetheless, she brought her weight down so low she ultimately died from it."[36]

No Simple Answers

Young people with eating disorders suffer—a lot. They do not choose to live a life that spirals out of control, nor do they want to be a slave to food obsessions. Even knowing that they are doing great harm to their bodies does not change the fact that their entire sense of self revolves around an addiction that is as powerful as any drug. No one understands this feeling more than Claudia Faniello, who is open and honest about her painful battle with bulimia when she talks to teenagers. And she does not hold back in giving them advice for conquering their eating disorder: "You have to stand up and fight the monster that is constantly in your brain and sucks up all your values and thoughts."[37]

Primary Source Quotes*

What Are Eating Disorders?

❝Both anorexia and bulimia are characterized by a morbid fear of gaining weight and losing control over eating.❞

—David H. Barlow and V. Mark Durand, *Abnormal Psychology: An Integrative Approach*. Belmont, CA: Wadsworth Cengage Learning, 2009.

Barlow is a professor of psychology and psychiatry at Boston University, and Durand is a professor of psychology at the University of South Florida in St. Petersburg.

❝Both anorexia and bulimia occur more frequently among girls and women than among boys and men. However, the prevalence of eating disorders among males may be underestimated because of the perception that eating disorders are a feminine malady.❞

— David R. Shaffer and Katherine Kipp, *Developmental Psychology: Childhood & Adolescence*. Belmont, CA: Wadsworth Cengage Learning, 2010.

Shaffer is a psychology professor at the University of Georgia and Kipp is a developmental psychology professor at Gainesville State University in Florida.

❝The incidence and prevalence of eating disorders in children and adolescents has increased significantly in recent decades.❞

—David S. Rosen, "Clinical Report—Identification and Management of Eating Disorders in Children and Adolescents," *Pediatrics*, December 2010. http://pediatrics.aappublications.org.

Rosen is an eating disorder specialist who is a professor in the Department of Psychiatry at the University of Michigan Medical School.

❝Perhaps one of the most important and startling things I learned both during my ten-year battle with an eating disorder and during my recovery is just how much ignorance, misinformation, fear and stigma are still attached to eating disorders even in the midst of the so-called information age.❞

—Johanna S. Kandel, *Life Beyond Your Eating Disorder*. New York: Harlequin, 2010.

Kandel, who suffered from an eating disorder for 10 years, is the founder and executive director of the Alliance for Eating Disorders Awareness.

❝When it comes to eating disorders and our youth, the trend is alarming. They are being diagnosed at a much younger age and more often.❞

Rakesh Ranjan, "Eating Disorders: Part III," *Medina Gazette*, April 21, 2010. http://medinagazette.northcoastnow.com.

Ranjan is a psychiatrist from Medina, Ohio.

❝Eating disorders are equal opportunity offenders that cross the barriers of race, education level and socio-economic status.❞

—Kimberly Dennis, "Is There Such a Thing as a Binge Eating Disorder?" DailyStrength, January 11, 2010. www.dailystrength.org.

Dennis is a psychiatrist and the medical director of Chicago's Timberline Knolls Residential Treatment Center.

66 Patients with bulimia are usually ashamed of their symptoms, whereas patients with anorexia nervosa may take pride in their sense of control to attain what they consider perfection. 99

—Kathryn J. Zerbe, interviewed by Randi Hutter Epstein, "Exploring Treatments for Eating Disorders," *New York Times*, July 13, 2009. www.nytimes.com.

Zerbe is a professor of psychiatry at Oregon Health and Science University and the author of several books about eating disorders.

66 I am in recovery from anorexia nervosa, major depression, self-injury, and bulimia. It is still difficult for me to say this aloud. The social taboos surrounding these mental illnesses are just as vicious as they ever were. 99

—Lucy Howard-Taylor, *Biting Anorexia: A Firsthand Account of an Internal War*. Oakland, CA: New Harbinger, 2009.

Howard-Taylor is a young woman from Canada who wrote about her struggles with eating disorders when she was 18 years old.

66 A binge is considered eating a larger amount of food than most people would eat under similar situations. For instance, when you have bulimia, you may eat an entire cake, rather than just a slice or two. And you may continue eating until you're painfully full. 99

—Mayo Clinic, "Bulimia Nervosa," February 23, 2010. www.mayoclinic.com.

The Mayo Clinic is a world-renowned medical facility headquartered in Rochester, Minnesota.

What Are Eating Disorders?

- Ohio psychiatrist Kathleen N. Franco states that eating disorders have been reported in up to **4 percent** of adolescents and young adults.

- The American Academy of Child & Adolescent Psychiatry states that as many as **10 percent** of girls and young women suffer from an eating disorder.

- According to the National Association of Anorexia Nervosa and Associated Disorders, more than **85 percent** of eating disorder sufferers report the onset of their illness before age 20.

- The National Institute of Mental Health estimates that males account for **5 to 15 percent** of patients with anorexia or bulimia.

- The South Carolina Department of Mental Health states that **74 percent** of American Indian girls report purging and taking diet pills to lose weight.

- The National Association of Anorexia Nervosa and Associated Disorders reports that among gay males, nearly **14 percent** suffer from bulimia and **20 percent** have anorexia.

- According to the University of Maryland Medical Center, a study of over 2,000 women found that **bulimia** (or a combination of bulimia and anorexia) was more common among women suffering from type 1 diabetes.

Prevalence Highest Among Older Teens, Girls

The exact prevalence of eating disorders among teenagers is not known because statistics are dependent on records of those who seek treatment. From data that have been gathered, however, it appears that eating disorders are more common among teenage girls aged 17 to 18.

Eating Disorder Prevalence in Teens

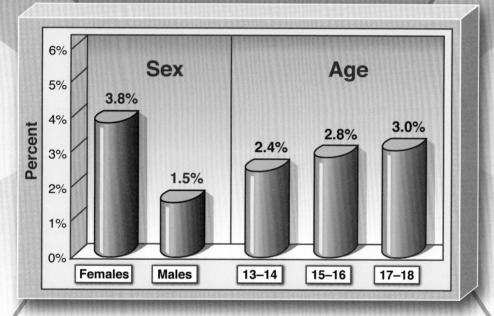

Source: National Institute of Mental Health, "Eating Disorders Among Children," July 29, 2010. www.nimh.nih.gov.

- Ohio psychiatrist Kathleen N. Franco says that the most common age for the onset of anorexia is in the mid-teens, with about **5 percent** of patients developing the disorder in their early twenties.

- According to Ohio psychiatrist Rakesh Ranjan, about **1 percent** of teenage girls suffer from anorexia, and approximately **5 percent** have bulimia.

Unhealthy Weight Loss Methods Used by Teens

Teens who go on diets, take diet pills, or even use laxatives or vomit on occasion, do not necessarily have an eating disorder. But health experts say that these actions can be the first step toward developing an eating disorder. In a survey conducted between September 2008 and December 2009, more than 16,000 high school students throughout the United States answered questions about their eating and dieting habits. This graph shows how they responded when asked about methods of trying to lose weight.

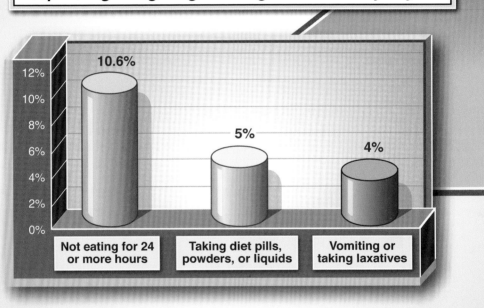

Percent of students who tried to lose weight or keep from gaining weight during the last 30 days by . . .

10.6%	5%	4%
Not eating for 24 or more hours	Taking diet pills, powders, or liquids	Vomiting or taking laxatives

Source: Centers for Disease Control and Prevention, "Youth Risk Behavior Surveillance—United States, 2009," *Morbidity and Mortality Weekly Report*, June 4, 2010. www.cdc.gov.

- A February 2010 article on the website WebMD states that most people with binge-eating disorder are either overweight or obese, meaning they are **20 to 30 percent** above their ideal weight.

- A July 2010 report by the National Eating Disorders Association states that a rise in incidence of **anorexia** among girls aged 15 to 19 has occurred in every decade since 1930.

- According to the Alliance for Eating Disorders Awareness, anorexia is the third most common **chronic illness** among adolescents.

- The Alliance for Eating Disorders Awareness states that **40 percent** of Americans have either suffered from an eating disorder or know someone who has.

- According to the National Association of Anorexia Nervosa and Associated Disorders, over **50 percent** of teenage girls and nearly **one-third** of teenage boys use unhealthy weight-control methods such as skipping meals, fasting, smoking cigarettes, vomiting, and abuse of laxatives.

Why Do Teenagers Develop Eating Disorders?

“Eating disorders are very complex, and despite scientific research to understand them, the biological, behavioral and social underpinnings of these illnesses remain elusive.”

—National Institute of Mental Health, the largest scientific organization in the world specializing in mental illness research and the promotion of mental health.

“Because of my genetic predisposition and perfectionistic traits, my once innocent diet developed into an eating disorder.”

—Johanna S. Kandel, who suffered from an eating disorder for 10 years, is the founder and executive director of the Alliance for Eating Disorders Awareness.

Medical science has yielded remarkable discoveries and achievements over the years. Researchers have found the cause of numerous diseases, and this has led to the development of preventative vaccines and lifesaving treatments. The same cannot be said of eating disorders, however, since no one knows what causes them. Yet even in the absence of a definitive cause, technological advances have greatly increased scientific understanding, including about the biological nature of eating disorders. Ovidio Bermudez, who is a psychiatrist from Tulsa, Oklahoma, writes: "This has facilitated the shift in public opinion from viewing eating disorders as lifestyle choices to recognizing them as serious mental illnesses." Bermudez adds a caveat, though: "There is much work to be done, and we still have more questions than answers."[38]

The Intrigue of Genetics

As scientists have continued to learn about eating disorders, they have become increasingly focused on the search for a cause. Because studies have consistently shown that eating disorders run in families, meaning they are hereditary, genetics has been—and will continue to be—a major focus of research. In order to know why this is important, it is necessary to have an understanding of the human genome, which is the body's genetic makeup.

The story of genetics begins with cells, which are the building blocks of life. The human body is made up of *tens of trillions* of cells, and within the nucleus of each (with the exception of red blood cells, which lack nuclei) are threadlike structures called chromosomes. Each chromosome is composed of long, tightly coiled molecules known as deoxyribonucleic acid, or DNA. Genes, from the Greek word *genos* meaning "origin" or "kin," are the basic units of heredity and are composed of DNA.

> **The simplest definition of genes is that they make people who they are.**

The simplest definition of genes is that they make people who they are. Genes are responsible for determining what color eyes someone has, as well as whether he or she is dark-skinned or fair, has a round- or oval-shaped face, is short or tall, and has straight or curly hair. If a particular gene has been altered in some way, it is known as a mutation and can result in a range of mental and physical problems. According to numerous scientists, this includes eating disorders, as Stanford University psychiatrist James Lock explains: "Clearly a genetic predisposition is a risk factor for developing an eating disorder—heritability estimates range from 25 to 75 percent in twin studies. Sociocultural factors also play a role, but since everyone is exposed to these and most don't develop an eating disorder, something more is involved."[39]

An Exciting Breakthrough

That "something more" refers to genetics. One of the twins studies mentioned by Lock was published in June 2010 by researchers from Michigan State and Florida State Universities. The focus was on the role that genetics might play in the development of eating disorders during adolescence, which occurs much more often than in adulthood. The team, led by Michigan State University psychologist Kelly Klump, studied 198 identical and fraternal twins aged 10 to 15 who were going through puberty. Klump's team discovered that the influence of genes was much greater in the girls who had especially high levels of a hormone known as estradiol, compared with those whose levels were normal. The primary form of the hormone estrogen, estradiol occurs naturally as girls reach puberty, and is responsible for growth of the female reproductive organs and breasts, as well as the regulation of bone development. Higher levels of estradiol could possibly explain why teenage girls are most susceptible to developing eating disorders.

Although the study's finding did not reveal which genes were being influenced by estradiol, Klump says knowing that the hormone is involved in the development of eating disorders could eventually open the door to new prevention and treatment methods. She explains: "The reason we see an increase in genetic influences during puberty is that the genes for disordered eating are essentially getting switched on during that time. This research was trying to figure out why. What's turning on the genes during puberty? And what we found is that increases in estradiol apparently are activating genetic risk for eating disorders."[40] Klump adds that more research is necessary in order to confirm her team's findings, as well as to explore the specific genes that might be affected by estradiol.

> The brain's role in the development of eating disorders has been of interest to scientists for years, and research has produced a number of important discoveries.

Clues Within the Brain

The brain is the most powerful organ in the human body. It functions as the body's master control center, regulating everything from thoughts, memories, and imagination to people's ability to speak, laugh, walk, dance, swallow, and even blink their eyes. Scientists have long suspected that eating disorders are at least partially caused by brain wiring that has gone awry, and numerous studies have strengthened that theory. According to Julie O'Toole, there is no question that eating disorders are biological illnesses of the brain. She says that just as the pancreas produces insulin and the thyroid gland produces thyroid hormone, the brain produces behavior: "Behavior is just the visible manifestation of many, many chemical processes in the brain."[41] O'Toole emphasizes that behavior needs to be viewed as a product of brain function, rather than the common assumption that it is volitional, or a conscious choice.

The brain's role in the development of eating disorders has been of interest to scientists for years, and research has produced a number of important discoveries. One study was published in 2009 by researchers from England and involved in-depth neurological testing on more than 200 anorexia sufferers, nearly all of whom were girls and young women. The team found that 70 percent of the participants had some sort of brain dysfunction that was likely sustained before they were born, when their brains were still developing. Some had damage to neurotransmitters, which are chemicals that enable brain cells to communicate with each other, while others had undergone subtle changes in the structure of their brains.

> " In the same way that sociocultural factors are not solely responsible, the reverse is also true—only a fraction of teens who are genetically predisposed to eating disorders go on to develop them. "

Ian Frampton, one of the study's authors, refers to this dysfunction as an "underlying vulnerability" among some adolescents that predisposes them to develop an eating disorder. He shares his thoughts about what he and his team discovered: "These findings could help us to understand this beguiling disease that we don't know how to treat."[42] A key benefit of the study, according to Frampton, is that it shows the significance of brain activity in the development of eating disorders, rather than solely attributing them to the family, the media's glamorization of super-thin celebrities, or other sociocultural factors. He explains: "Those things are important but there must be other factors, involving genetics and science, that make some young people much more vulnerable than others."[43]

The Role of Family

The evidence connecting genetics and brain chemistry with eating disorders is indeed compelling, and few would dispute the importance of that connection. But in the same way that sociocultural factors are not solely responsible, the reverse is also true—only a fraction of teens who are genetically predisposed to eating disorders go on to develop them. Consequently, most scientists believe that the disorders do not have a singular cause but rather result from a complex interaction of biological and environmental factors. Mental health professionals often refer to this as biology loading the gun and environment pulling the trigger.

One of the greatest sources of controversy is whether a teen's eating disorder may be related to family environment. While many teens who suffer from eating disorders come from close, loving families, not everyone has that advantage. Many eating disorder specialists say that a dysfunctional family environment can be a factor in the development of an eating disorder, serving as the trigger for someone who is biologically vulnerable. As the Mayo Clinic writes: "People who feel less secure in their families, whose parents and siblings may be overly critical, or whose families tease them about their appearance are at higher risk of eating disorders."[44]

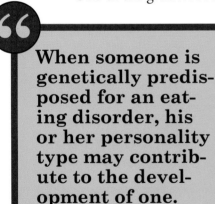

> **When someone is genetically predisposed for an eating disorder, his or her personality type may contribute to the development of one.**

Anna Paterson's childhood is a prime example of how a vulnerable child's family environment can trigger an eating disorder. She writes: "It is likely that my life would have been very different if I had been born a boy. My grandmother liked her grandsons but not her new granddaughter. The abuse began at the age of three and it continued throughout my life at regular intervals."[45] Paterson's grandmother was a major influence throughout her childhood and adolescence, and no matter what Paterson did, the older woman never approved. Nor did Paterson feel like she could ever please her parents. "My self-esteem dropped dramatically," she says, "and I believed that everything bad that happened was my fault. I did not think that anyone loved me and wanted to just disappear."[46]

In response to her emotional pain, Paterson stopped eating when she was a teenager, and her weight began to plummet. By the time she was 21, she had become so emaciated that she was seriously ill: "My body was starving hungry and so I became obsessed with food. It occupied my thoughts during every waking moment and then I would sleep fitfully with relentless nightmares."[47] But even as her body wasted away, she received neither sympathy nor support from her family. In fact, her parents blamed her for having anorexia and accused her of ruining their lives. "The guilt I felt was tremendous," she says, "although I still could not force myself to eat. By now, eating had become a terrifying prospect for me."[48]

Never Good Enough

When someone is genetically predisposed for an eating disorder, his or her personality type may contribute to the development of one. For instance, it is common among teens who have anorexia and/or bulimia to be extreme, intense perfectionists. Author Aimee Liu, whose long battle with anorexia began when she was a teenager, says that perfectionism is a consistent trait among those with eating disorders. She writes:

> Most people who have had an eating disorder believe down to their nerve endings that perfection is a real, attainable noble state and that it is their right and duty to claim it, whether they are performing in a play, organizing a closet, planning a party, or anticipating a date. They probably can't tell you why they feel this way, but the ultimate standard nevertheless shadows them like a malevolent conscience.[49]

Allison Kreiger Walsh can certainly relate to Liu's account of perfectionism. Except for those who personally know the former Miss Florida, people who see Walsh today would have no idea that she fought an excruciating battle with bulimia throughout high school. She says that a major factor was her relentless drive to be perfect in every way. She writes: "From the very beginning, I was a complete perfectionist and put a lot of pressure on myself. From pushing myself in the gym to expecting straight As on my report card, I didn't want to settle for anything less than the best."[50]

Before Walsh was stricken with bulimia, she was a dancer and a champion baton twirler, had many friends, and was popular in school—then her eating disorder robbed her of everything. She became so obsessed with food that she planned her entire day around bingeing and purging. By the time she was a senior, she was forcing herself to vomit 10 to 12 times a day, and was also suffering from anorexia. Her symptoms were very visible and her health was deteriorating at a rapid pace, as she explains: "I was extremely weak, I had lost half the hair on my head, I had broken blood vessels in my eyes, I had done damage to my esophagus from the bingeing and purging, I couldn't digest food properly even if I wanted to, and I was at a dangerously low weight."[51] Knowing she could no longer go on that way, Walsh turned to her parents for help and got into a treatment program.

Uncertainties Abound

With all the studies that have been done, and all the knowledge that scientists have gained, eating disorders are still bewildering mental illnesses for which the cause remains unknown. It is widely believed that these disorders result from a complex interaction of genetics, brain chemistry, and sociocultural factors. As research continues, scientists may eventually be more certain about the cause of eating disorders, rather than being reliant on theories.

Why Do Teenagers Develop Eating Disorders?

66 **When people think about eating disorders, they often think that they are a choice, but that simply isn't true. Eating disorders are not choices; they are mental illnesses.** 99

—Allison Kreiger Walsh, "Profile in Recovery: Allison's Story," in *Life Beyond Your Eating Disorder*, by Johanna S. Kandel. New York: Harlequin, 2010.

Walsh is a former Miss Florida who struggled with anorexia and bulimia as a teenager.

66 **Eating disorders have complex causes and can't be willed away.** 99

—Alliance for Eating Disorders Awareness, "Debunking Eating Disorder Myths," 2010. www.allianceforeatingdisorders.com.

The Alliance for Eating Disorders Awareness seeks to educate the public about the dangers of eating disorders and reduce the rate and severity of these disorders among people of all ages.

* Editor's Note: While the definition of a primary source can be narrowly or broadly defined, for the purposes of Compact Research, a primary source consists of: 1) results of original research presented by an organization or researcher; 2) eyewitness accounts of events, personal experience, or work experience; 3) first-person editorials offering pundits' opinions; 4) government officials presenting political plans and/or policies; 5) representatives of organizations presenting testimony or policy.

66 **Family, twin, and molecular genetic studies are demonstrating a substantial role for genetic factors in the development of the eating disorders, although there is uncertainty regarding the size of the genetic versus environmental contributions.** 99

—S. Hossein Fatemi and Paula J. Clayton, eds., *The Medical Basis of Psychiatry*. Totowa, NJ: Humana, 2008.

Fatemi is a psychiatrist from Minneapolis, and Clayton is with the American Foundation for Suicide Prevention.

66 **Some researchers claim that there is a genetic link— that eating disorders are passed down from parents to their children. But this theory is relatively new and hasn't been well researched.** 99

Evelyn Resh, *The Secret Lives of Teen Girls: What Your Mother Wouldn't Talk About but Your Daughter Needs to Know*. Carlsbad, CA: Hay House, 2009.

Resh is a certified nurse-midwife who specializes in the treatment of teenage girls.

66 **Too often adolescents define themselves in relation to unhealthy role models and body types. For girls we know these body types are based on emaciated models. For boys these body types are based on muscular and cut physiques that are unnaturally induced or impossible to sustain.** 99

Paul Hokemeyer, "Male Eating Disorders," *The Dr. Oz Show*, September 9, 2010. www.doctoroz.com.

Hokemeyer is a marriage and family therapist from New York City.

66 **The causes of the various disorders aren't known, but it seems indisputable that the current Western emphasis on slimness as a mark of feminine attractiveness contributes greatly.** 99

—University of Pittsburgh Medical Center, "Eating Disorders," August 2010. www.upmc.com.

The University of Pittsburgh Medical Center is a leading health-care facility headquartered in Pittsburgh, Pennsylvania.

66 If only I had known that Anna was vulnerable to developing an eating disorder because of her genetic makeup, her personality traits, and the culture she grew up in, I may have been able to intervene before she developed a full-blown eating disorder.**99**

—Kitty Westin, foreword to Sari Fine Shepphird, *100 Questions & Answers About Anorexia Nervosa*. Sudbury, MA: Jones and Bartlett, 2010.

Westin, whose daughter developed anorexia when she was 16 and later died, is president of the Eating Disorders Coalition for Research, Policy & Action.

66 We are far from knowing specific genes that cause eating disorders. There are a number of genes that work with environmental triggers. Dieting and loss of weight may influence the development of anorexia by turning on a gene that may influence an eating disorder.**99**

—Thomas Insel, "General Information: What Causes Eating Disorders?" National Association of Anorexia Nervosa and Associated Disorders, 2010. www.anad.org.

Insel is the director of the National Institute of Mental Health.

66 People with different cultural backgrounds may develop eating disorders because it's hard to adapt to a new culture (a theory called 'culture clash'). The stress of trying to live in two different cultures may cause some minorities to develop their eating disorders.**99**

—The National Women's Health Information Center, *Anorexia Nervosa*, June 15, 2009. www.womenshealth.gov.

The National Women's Health Information Center is dedicated to improving the health and well-being of all women and girls in the United States.

Why Do Teenagers Develop Eating Disorders?

- According to the Eating Disorders Coalition for Research, Policy & Action, the risk of developing an eating disorder is from **50 to 80 percent** determined by genetics.

- The National Women's Health Information Center states that traumatic incidents such as **abuse or rape** can lead to the onset of an eating disorder.

- Studies have shown that in most cases, the unhealthy overeating habits that develop into binge-eating disorder begin during childhood, often as a result of **learned eating habits**.

- The American Academy of Family Physicians says that in some people with eating disorders, the **hypothalamus** (the part of the brain that controls appetite) may fail to send proper signals about hunger and fullness.

- According to the Alliance for Eating Disorders Awareness, the most common behavior that will lead to an eating disorder is **dieting**.

- National Institute of Mental Health director Thomas Insel states that in adolescents who develop eating disorders, those labeled as **"severe dieters"** had an 18 times greater chance of developing an eating disorder, with a 5 times greater chance for moderate dieters.

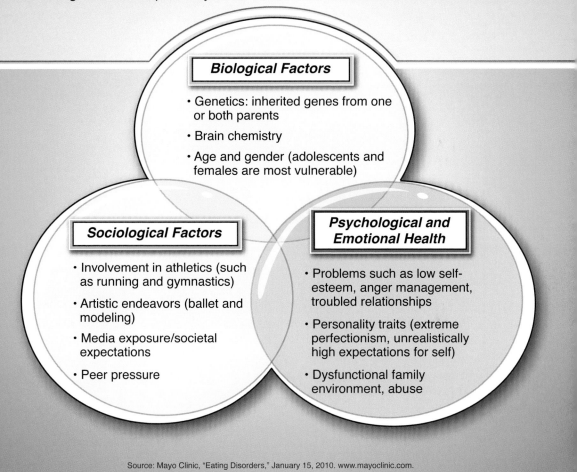

Possible Causes of Eating Disorders

Scientists cannot say with any certainty what causes teenagers to develop eating disorders. Genetics, brain chemistry, emotional health, and sociocultural influences are all thought to play a part by working together in complex ways.

Biological Factors

- Genetics: inherited genes from one or both parents
- Brain chemistry
- Age and gender (adolescents and females are most vulnerable)

Sociological Factors

- Involvement in athletics (such as running and gymnastics)
- Artistic endeavors (ballet and modeling)
- Media exposure/societal expectations
- Peer pressure

Psychological and Emotional Health

- Problems such as low self-esteem, anger management, troubled relationships
- Personality traits (extreme perfectionism, unrealistically high expectations for self)
- Dysfunctional family environment, abuse

Source: Mayo Clinic, "Eating Disorders," January 15, 2010. www.mayoclinic.com.

- According to the National Women's Health Information Center, **parents who think looks are important**, diet themselves, or criticize their children's bodies are more likely to have a child who develops anorexia or bulimia.

Teen Girls Want to Be Thinner

The media are often criticized for placing so much focus on ultra-skinny fashion models and celebrities because of the potential effect this can have on young people, especially girls. Although publicity cannot, by itself, cause eating disorders, mental health experts warn that constant exposure to such images can influence young people to take drastic measures to emulate their idols, which could trigger the onset of an eating disorder. This graph shows how more than 1,000 teenage girls responded to a February 2010 joint survey by the Girl Scouts and Dove Self-Esteem Fund when asked questions about models who are featured in fashion magazines.

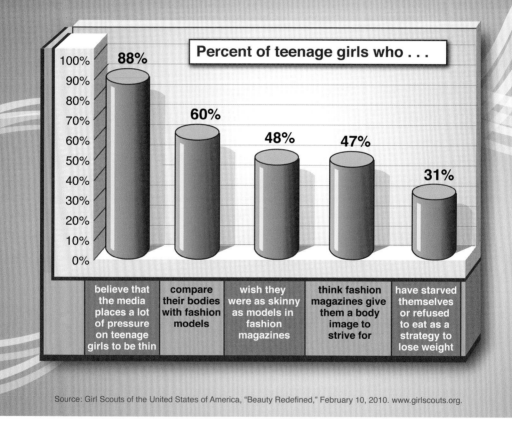

Source: Girl Scouts of the United States of America, "Beauty Redefined," February 10, 2010. www.girlscouts.org.

- Some studies suggest that the brain chemical **serotonin**, which regulates mood and is associated with anxiety and some compulsive behaviors, may play a role in eating disorders.

- Studies have shown that young women who have **type 1 diabetes** have an increased risk of developing eating disorders.

- According to the National Association of Anorexia Nervosa and Associated Disorders, **69 percent** of girls in fifth to twelfth grade reported that magazine pictures influenced their idea of a perfect body shape.

- Mental health experts say that personality traits such as low self-esteem, unhappiness with appearance, extreme perfectionism, inability to express anger and frustration, and the tendency to set unrealistic goals for oneself, can be **risk factors** for the development of eating disorders.

- In a February 2010 survey by the Girl Scouts of America, **47 percent** of teen girl respondents said that fashion magazines gave them a body image to strive for.

What Are the
Dangers of
Eating Disorders?

"It is important to emphasize that eating disorders can be medically dangerous and that medical problems can result in death."

—National Association of Anorexia Nervosa and Associated Disorders, which seeks to prevent and alleviate the problems of eating disorders.

"Teen eating disorders can cause serious and even life-threatening health problems."

—Mayo Clinic, a world-renowned medical facility headquartered in Rochester, Minnesota.

In early January 2009, 15-year-old Anna Wood decided to lose a few pounds that she had gained over the holidays. This was certainly nothing out of the ordinary, as many people do the same thing at the beginning of a new year. In fact, Wood's mother, Christine Gibson, went on the diet along with her daughter. After about 5 or 6 weeks, Gibson was satisfied with her weight and decided to resume eating normally—but Wood was not finished yet. She liked the fact that she had lost weight, and it gave her the incentive to lose even more. At the time, neither she nor her mother had any way of knowing that Wood was at the beginning of a downward spiral that would ultimately kill her.

At first Gibson did not think much about her daughter's determination to become thinner, as she assumed it would not last. But she became concerned when Wood's eating habits started to change drastically. Gibson tried to persuade her to eat, but the girl wanted no part of it. To appease her mother, Wood began using tricks to make it look like she was eating. "She became deceptive and sneaky," says Gibson. "She would hide food up her sleeve and throw it away when I wasn't looking. She'd also been making herself sick."[52] Just over a year later, Wood had a heart attack and died. What had started as a postholiday diet had developed into anorexia, and the disease ravaged her young body. Along with destroying her heart, it caused all her other vital organs to shut down, and she was both brain damaged and paralyzed. "It just happened so quickly," says Gibson, "from realising she had anorexia to her passing away. . . . We were heartbroken."[53]

> **The majority of young people who suffer from eating disorders do not die from them. But the stark reality is, these disorders do have the potential to kill.**

Wood's tragic story is one of anorexia at its most extreme, when a teen has literally starved herself to death. Not everyone reaches that point, of course. The majority of young people who suffer from eating disorders do not die from them. But the stark reality is, these disorders do have the potential to kill. Collectively, they have the highest death rate of all mental illnesses, including major depression. Anorexia alone claims the lives of up to 20 percent of those who suffer from it, and the longer someone has the disorder, the greater the likelihood that he or she will die from it. Anorexia also has a very high suicide risk. According to the University of Maryland Medical Center, as many as half of the deaths associated with anorexia involve sufferers taking their own lives.

Wreaking Havoc on the Body

Whether through the self-starvation of anorexia or the repeated purging of bulimia, the body takes a terrible beating. Dehydration, which occurs when someone takes in fewer fluids than the body loses, is one of the primary dangers of these eating disorders. Anorexics deprive their bodies of nutrients from food, and bulimics lose nutrients through vomiting and/or the abuse of laxatives and diuretics. Susan Schulherr writes: "All foods contain nutritious fluids that cannot be compensated for by drinking water alone. Severely limiting the intake of nutrients and fluids over time causes your body to become dehydrated. Severely restricting carbohydrates and fats can also result in dehydration."[54]

One of the most dangerous effects of dehydration is that it disrupts and reduces the levels of electrolytes in the body. Essential mineral salts, such as sodium, potassium, calcium, chloride, magnesium, phosphate, and sulfate, change into electrolytes when they dissolve in the body's fluids. Electrolytes are so named because they have the ability to conduct electricity, meaning they trigger electrical impulses that enable cells to send messages back and forth among themselves. These electrical charges stimulate the heart to beat, as well as regulate the function of all body organs, including muscles and nerves. Another function of electrolytes is to assist the body in maintaining normal fluid levels.

> **When dehydration depletes the body of fluids, this reduces the levels of essential minerals and can lead to an electrolyte imbalance—which can kill someone very quickly.**

When dehydration depletes the body of fluids, this reduces the levels of essential minerals and can lead to an electrolyte imbalance—which can kill someone very quickly. For instance, calcium and potassium are the electrolytes that are in control of the heart, and they are crucial for a regular heartbeat and normal heart function. Schulherr describes what happens when they are deficient: "Electrolyte imbalances can result in sudden cardiac arrest and permanent heart damage or death. An early symptom of dehydration and an electrolyte imbalance is irregular heart rhythm. Left untreated, deadly results can follow."[55] In addition to heart damage, electrolyte imbalances can cause seizures; damage or destroy the kidneys, liver, and brain; and potentially cause paralysis ranging in severity from weak muscles to complete loss of all ability to move.

Disintegrating Bones

In the same way that eating disorders starve the body of nutrients, they deprive bones of minerals that are essential for strength and growth. This is especially damaging to teenagers because adolescence is a crucial time for the development of bone mass that should last throughout a person's life. Diane Mickley, an eating disorder specialist who is president of the National Eating Disorders Association, explains: "There's a narrow window of time to accrue bone mass to last a lifetime. You're supposed to be pouring in bone, and you're losing it instead."[56] Mickley adds that such bone loss can happen rapidly—within six months after self-starvation begins—and it is one of the most irreversible complications of anorexia. According to the University of Maryland Medical Center, up to two-thirds of children and adolescents with the disorder fail to develop strong bones during their critical growing period.

> Once a teen has developed osteopenia, it becomes increasingly unlikely that he or she will be able to accumulate normal amounts of bone mass.

An estimated 90 percent of anorexia sufferers develop a condition known as osteopenia, which is reduced bone density due to loss of minerals. Once a teen has developed osteopenia, it becomes increasingly unlikely that he or she will be able to accumulate normal amounts of bone mass. In the book *The Parent's Guide to Eating Disorders*, authors Marcia Herrin and Nancy Matsumoto note that adolescent anorexia patients lose more bone than adults with anorexia. They write: "As the anorexic girl or boy matures, the risk that the low bone mass of osteopenia will progress to osteoporosis increases."[57]

At their young age, teenagers may not think much about the bone disease known as osteoporosis, and if they do, it is likely because of a mother, grandmother, or aunt who suffers from it. It is, after all, a condition that is usually associated with older women who have gone through menopause. But as the self-starvation of anorexia continues to deprive bones of crucial minerals, osteoporosis can strike during the teenage years. This is what happened to Johanna S. Kandel after her struggle with anorexia and bulimia. Kandel was only 17 years old when the doctor informed her that she suffered from full-blown osteoporosis. Although the disease's severity varies from person to person, it can be debilitating. Over time, it can result in a hump on the back, a permanent stoop, and loss of height—a person actually shrinks and becomes shorter. People with osteoporosis often suffer from chronic, severe pain, and their bones become so thin and brittle that they fracture easily.

Starving the Heart

Both anorexia and bulimia can severely damage the body's vital organs, often due to electrolyte imbalances. But the self-starvation of anorexia can also starve the life out of major organs. That is because the body creates its own energy by breaking down carbohydrates from foods into glucose (blood sugar), and then burning the glucose as fuel. If someone does not consume enough food, the body begins to break fat down to make up for the loss of glucose. And when an anorexia sufferer has starved to the point of having no fat left, the body will continue to find the fuel it needs—by devouring its own muscle.

This can be devastating to every organ of the body, but is particularly dangerous to the heart. As the body continues to lose muscle mass, the heart muscle shrinks in size (a condition known as cardiac atrophy), growing progressively weaker as it wastes away. Mickley explains: "The cardiac tolls are acute and significant, and set in quickly."[58] Finally, the heart has sustained so much damage that it simply gives out and stops beating.

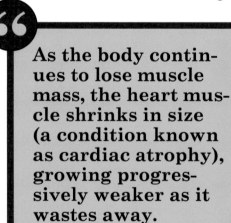

> As the body continues to lose muscle mass, the heart muscle shrinks in size (a condition known as cardiac atrophy), growing progressively weaker as it wastes away.

A rare heart complication associated with self-starvation is known as mitral valve prolapse. This condition develops because even though the heart itself shrinks, the valves inside the heart do not. As Herrin and Matsumoto write: "The result is a set of misshapen valves that do not close properly. The faulty valves cause blood to leak back into the heart chamber, which in turn causes palpitations [rapid, irregular heartbeat] and chest pain."[59] They add that mitral valve prolapse can sometimes be reversed if the sufferer regains weight, but it is a potentially life-threatening condition.

Playing with Fire

Studies have shown that anorexia and bulimia are especially common among females with type 1 diabetes, a disease in which the immune system attacks insulin-producing cells in the pancreas. This causes the body to produce little or no insulin, a hormone that helps regulate the levels of glucose in the bloodstream. Those who suffer from diabetes must take daily shots of insulin, and their survival depends on it. Coping with the disease can be tough, especially for teenagers, as Cedars-Sinai Medical Center physician Ruchi Mathur writes: "There is the issue of dealing with a chronic illness and the fear that goes along with learning about the potential complications. Many younger patients also have issues with body image. 'My injection sites make me look lumpy.' 'This whole needle thing is disgusting—look at my bruises.' 'I have diabetes—my body is different from everyone else's.'"[60]

One of the most difficult aspects of diabetes for young people is that regularly injecting insulin into the body causes weight gain. In an effort to keep their weight down, diabetic teens sometimes resort to drastic measures, as Mathur explains: "While insulin keeps their muscle mass from breaking down, it also encourages fat storage. As a result, patients learn to manipulate their insulin—often skipping doses in an attempt to reduce weight gain. The term for this condition is 'Diabulimia.'" This is a risky practice, as Mathur adds: "The repercussions of manipulating insulin in such a manner can be enormous."[61] Although diabulimia is not officially recognized as an eating disorder, awareness of the condition is growing—and so is its prevalence, especially among teenage girls. This trend is very disturbing to medical professionals because diabulimia can be deadly.

When someone with diabetes deliberately reduces his or her insulin intake, the body's cells are deprived of the glucose needed for energy so they begin to burn fat—which creates a dangerous situation for a diabetic. As the body consumes fat, this results in the production of toxic acidic chemicals known as ketones, which build up in the bloodstream and can poison the body. When levels of ketones get too high, the person can develop a condition known as ketoacidosis—and the resulting damage to the body can be catastrophic. Ketoacidosis can interfere with the kidneys' ability to filter out impurities from the body and can cause them to fail, as well as contribute to diseases of the eye that can lead to blindness. At its very worst, ketoacidosis can send someone into a diabetic coma and cause death.

Pain and Suffering

Eating disorders take a disastrous toll on the health of those who suffer from them. When the body is deprived of essential nutrients, the result can be deadly electrolyte imbalances and eventual organ failure. Osteopenia may lead to the bone-destroying disease osteoporosis, causing sufferers a lifetime of pain. The little-known condition known as diabulimia can do disastrous damage to the body, ranging from eye disease and blindness to kidney damage and death. Offering the perspective of someone who has lived through an eating disorder and knows from personal experience how devastating it can be, Anna Paterson writes: "Eating disorders cause a great deal of physical and mental damage. When you are suffering from one of these illnesses, it can often feel like a life sentence."[62]

Primary Source Quotes*

What Are the Dangers of Eating Disorders?

66 **Multiple organ failure: That's right; with enough deprivation, all the organs in your body can close up shop and quit functioning.** 99

—Susan Schulherr, *Eating Disorders for Dummies*. Hoboken, NJ: Wiley, 2008.

Schulherr is a psychotherapist from New York City who specializes in eating disorders.

....

66 **Eating disorders can cause many dangerous medical and mental illnesses.** 99

—Kyla Boyse, "Eating Disorders: What Families Need to Know," YourChild: Development & Behavior Resources, University of Michigan, October 2010. www.med.umich.edu.

Boyse is a registered nurse with the University of Michigan Health System.

....

* Editor's Note: While the definition of a primary source can be narrowly or broadly defined, for the purposes of Compact Research, a primary source consists of: 1) results of original research presented by an organization or researcher; 2) eyewitness accounts of events, personal experience, or work experience; 3) first-person editorials offering pundits' opinions; 4) government officials presenting political plans and/or policies; 5) representatives of organizations presenting testimony or policy.

❝Re-feeding syndrome can manifest as mental confusion, seizures, muscle weakness, difficulty breathing and cardiac arrest. . . . It is a particularly ironic and tragic way for a patient with anorexia nervosa to die, because it is caused by the medicine that will also cure: food.❞

— Julie O'Toole, "Risks of Re-Feeding Syndrome in Eating Disorder Treatment," Kartini Clinic, January 24, 2011. www.kartiniclinic.com.

O'Toole is a pediatrician and the founder of the Kartini Clinic for Disordered Eating in Portland, Oregon.

❝Anorexia is the most lethal of all psychiatric illnesses.❞

—Andrea D. Vazzana, interviewed by Laurie Barclay, "Eating Disorders: An Expert Interview with Andrea D. Vazzana, Ph.D.," Medscape, March 6, 2009. www.medscape.com.

Vazzana is a clinical assistant professor of child and adolescent psychiatry at New York University.

❝Many physical conditions result from the purging aspect of [bulimia], including electrolyte imbalances, gastrointestinal problems, and oral and tooth-related problems.❞

National Institute of Mental Health, "Bulimia Nervosa," August 5, 2010. www.nimh.nih.gov.

The National Institute of Mental Health is the largest scientific organization in the world specializing in mental illness research and the promotion of mental health.

❝When the heart is undergoing stress, electrolyte abnormalities can trigger arrhythmias. A starving body attacks its own muscle tissue in an effort to stay alive. In the case of extreme starvation, the heart simply stops.❞

Remuda Ranch, "Medical Complications of Anorexia Nervosa," 2010. www.remudaranch.com.

Remuda Ranch is a medical facility that treats women, adolescents, and children suffering from anorexia, bulimia, and anxiety disorders.

66 Research has shown that people with binge eating disorder report more health problems, stress, loss of sleep and suicidal thoughts than people without an eating disorder do. 99

—Center for Eating Disorders at Sheppard Pratt, "Eating Out of Control: Understanding Binge Eating Disorder," 2010. www.eatingdisorder.org.

Located in Baltimore, Maryland, the Center for Eating Disorders offers comprehensive, individualized care for children, adolescents, and adults with serious eating disorders.

66 Even with successful treatment of the eating disorder, osteoporosis may remain as a medical concern, primarily for patients with anorexia. Dental erosions are most often seen in patients with bulimia, but remain a concern for any patient who purges by vomiting. 99

—Pamela M. Williams, Jeffrey Goodie, and Charles D. Motsinger, "Treating Eating Disorders in Primary Care," *American Family Physician*, January 2008. www.aafp.org.

Williams, Goodie, and Motsinger are physicians from Bethesda, Maryland, and officers with the US Air Force.

66 Most of the medical complications of eating disorders resolve with refeeding and/or resolution of purging. However, there is increasing concern that some complications—particularly growth retardation, structural brain changes, and low bone mineral density—may, with time, become irreversible. 99

David S. Rosen, "Clinical Report—Identification and Management of Eating Disorders in Children and Adolescents," *Pediatrics*, December 2010. http://pediatrics.aappublications.org.

Rosen is an eating disorder specialist who is a professor in the Department of Psychiatry at the University of Michigan Medical School.

Facts and Illustrations

What Are the Dangers of Eating Disorders?

- According to the University of Maryland Medical Center, teens suffering from anorexia and/or bulimia are at high risk for developing **anxiety and depression** in young adulthood.

- Eating disorders have the **highest fatality rate** of all mental illnesses, including major depression.

- According to the National Institute of Mental Health, the **mortality rate** for females aged 15 to 24 who suffer from anorexia is about **12 times higher** than the annual death rate due to all causes for this age group.

- New York City psychologist Andrea D. Vazzana says that as many as **25 percent** of people with anorexia die as a result of the disorder, including an estimated **5 percent** who commit suicide.

- The University of Maryland Medical Center states that up to **two-thirds** of children and adolescent girls with anorexia fail to develop strong bones during their critical growing period.

- According to Pennsylvania psychologist Heidi Dalzell, about **one-third** of diabetics between the ages of 15 and 30 engage in the dangerous practice of manipulating their insulin in an effort to lose weight.

Health Problems Associated with Eating Disorders

Numerous health risks, many of which are life threatening, are associated with eating disorders. This was the focus of a study published in April 2009 by the Agency for Healthcare Research and Quality, which analyzed 6,012 patients (including teenagers) diagnosed with one or more eating disorder. As this graph indicates the most prevalent reason for hospitalization was fluid and electrolyte imbalances, which can cause rapid heart failure.

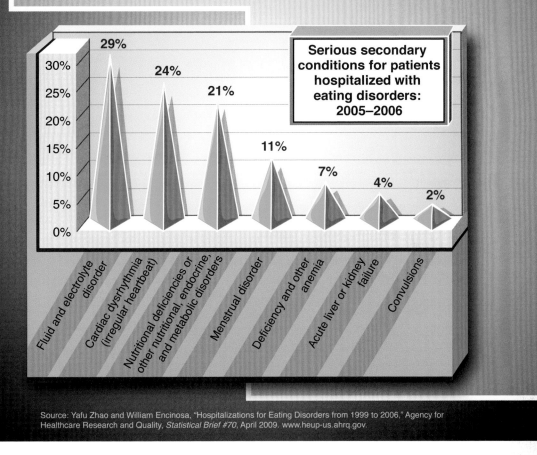

Serious secondary conditions for patients hospitalized with eating disorders: 2005–2006

- Fluid and electrolyte disorder: 29%
- Cardiac dysrhythmia (irregular heartbeat): 24%
- Nutritional deficiencies or other nutritional, endocrine, and metabolic disorders: 21%
- Menstrual disorder: 11%
- Deficiency and other anemia: 7%
- Acute liver or kidney failure: 4%
- Convulsions: 2%

Source: Yafu Zhao and William Encinosa, "Hospitalizations for Eating Disorders from 1999 to 2006," Agency for Healthcare Research and Quality, *Statistical Brief #70*, April 2009. www.heup-us.ahrq.gov.

- At its most severe, anorexia can cause the sufferer's **bone marrow** to dramatically reduce production of blood cells, which can result in a life-threatening condition called **pancytopenia**.

Anorexia and Bulimia Harm the Entire Body

Among teenagers, anorexia and bulimia are the most common eating disorders. They can wreak havoc on the body, causing physical problems that range from constipation and/or skin that bruises easily to dehydration, deadly electrolyte imbalances, and complete organ failure.

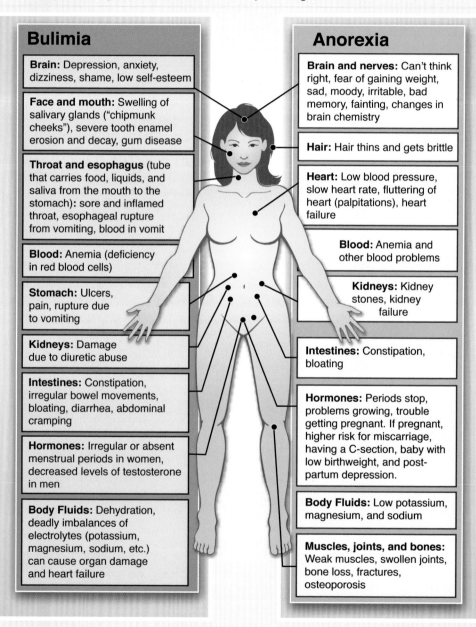

Bulimia

Brain: Depression, anxiety, dizziness, shame, low self-esteem

Face and mouth: Swelling of salivary glands ("chipmunk cheeks"), severe tooth enamel erosion and decay, gum disease

Throat and esophagus (tube that carries food, liquids, and saliva from the mouth to the stomach): sore and inflamed throat, esophageal rupture from vomiting, blood in vomit

Blood: Anemia (deficiency in red blood cells)

Stomach: Ulcers, pain, rupture due to vomiting

Kidneys: Damage due to diuretic abuse

Intestines: Constipation, irregular bowel movements, bloating, diarrhea, abdominal cramping

Hormones: Irregular or absent menstrual periods in women, decreased levels of testosterone in men

Body Fluids: Dehydration, deadly imbalances of electrolytes (potassium, magnesium, sodium, etc.) can cause organ damage and heart failure

Anorexia

Brain and nerves: Can't think right, fear of gaining weight, sad, moody, irritable, bad memory, fainting, changes in brain chemistry

Hair: Hair thins and gets brittle

Heart: Low blood pressure, slow heart rate, fluttering of heart (palpitations), heart failure

Blood: Anemia and other blood problems

Kidneys: Kidney stones, kidney failure

Intestines: Constipation, bloating

Hormones: Periods stop, problems growing, trouble getting pregnant. If pregnant, higher risk for miscarriage, having a C-section, baby with low birthweight, and post-partum depression.

Body Fluids: Low potassium, magnesium, and sodium

Muscles, joints, and bones: Weak muscles, swollen joints, bone loss, fractures, osteoporosis

Source: US Department of Health and Human Services, Office on Women's Health, "Anorexia Nervosa," "Bulimia Nervosa," June 15, 2009. www.womenshealth.gov.

- New York psychotherapist Susan Schulherr says that as many as **50 percent** of young women with bulimia have irregular menstrual periods.

- Nearly **90 percent** of females with anorexia experience **osteopenia**, which is loss of bone minerals, and **40 percent** develop **osteoporosis**, a more advanced and severe loss of bone density.

- According to the National Association for Anorexia Nervosa and Associated Disorders, the **mortality rate** associated with anorexia is **12 times higher** than the death rate associated with all causes of death for females 15-24 years old.

- The National Eating Disorders Association states that up to **89 percent** of bulimia patients show signs of tooth erosion, usually caused by repeated vomiting.

- According to the National Institutes of Health, frequent vomiting by those who suffer from bulimia sends **stomach acid** into the esophagus, which can cause permanent damage.

- The Weight-Control Information Network states that the obesity that typically results from binge-eating disorder can lead to **diabetes, high blood pressure, high blood cholesterol levels, gallbladder disease, heart disease, and certain types of cancer.**

Can Teenagers Overcome Eating Disorders?

We need to always keep the belief alive that recovery is possible, that no recovery is 'perfect' and no one should ever give up.

—Adrienne Ressler, president of the International Association of Eating Disorders Professionals.

Because of the destructive nature of the psychological and physical problems often associated with eating disorders, these disorders represent some of the most difficult psychiatric illnesses to treat.

—National Association of Anorexia Nervosa and Associated Disorders.

There was a time in Johanna S. Kandel's life when she simply could not imagine giving up her eating disorder. She felt as though her entire identity revolved around it, and to let it go would be like losing an important part of herself. But after watching her health continue to deteriorate, Kandel finally acknowledged how sick she was and that she needed help. Assisted by a team of medical and psychological professionals, she began to see that her attachment to the eating disorder was a product of the illness itself—and that her life depended on overcoming it. For the first time, Kandel desperately wanted to get better. After battling her eating disorder for so long, she was "sick and tired of being sick and tired." She explains:

> I wanted to thrive, not just barely survive. I wanted to laugh, I wanted to be present. My eating disorder stole 10 years of my life, and I wanted more. My eating disorder tore my family apart and stole friendships from me. I had people close to me that had lost their battle and I didn't want to die. I was tired of being in the "passenger seat" in my car of life. I knew that recovery meant climbing over the center console and getting in the driver's seat (with both hands on the wheel). Although I was so . . . scared, I was finally ready to live.[63]

Conquering Fears

Kandel was able to start healing because she knew that recovery depended on her willingness to change. But for a teen to acknowledge that an eating disorder is a serious, life-threatening problem is far from easy. For many, choosing recovery can be terrifying, even more so than continuing to battle an eating disorder. Kandel was willing to make the necessary changes to begin recovering—but she did not reach that point until she had struggled with her eating disorder for more than a decade.

When Kandel was still in the clutches of both anorexia and bulimia, she saw a number of different therapists and nutritionists who tried to help her, but she had no desire to help herself. She told the therapists "exactly what I knew they wanted to hear," and she was neither ready nor willing to imagine life without her eating disorder. She writes: "I manipulated everyone and sabotaged myself in order to maintain my eating disorder, which felt safe to me. The thought of giving up the eating disorder and going into an unknown place was much more frightening than maintaining the familiar, miserable as it was, and suffering the consequences."[64]

> " For many [teens], choosing recovery can be terrifying, even more so than continuing to battle an eating disorder. "

Many teens feel exactly the same way about their eating disorders, and one of the biggest reasons is their fear of gaining weight. After spending so long as a prisoner of their disorder, doing everything possible to keep from "getting fat," the idea of intentionally putting on pounds can seem overwhelming—as well as appalling. This is often a source of disbelief for the family and close friends of an eating disorder sufferer, who think that the person should *just start eating*. Cecily FitzGerald, an emergency physician who also treats patients with eating disorders, encounters this quite often. "Why won't she just eat the sandwich?" is a typical question asked by parents and other loved ones. Her response? "She can no more eat that sandwich than you can eat that shoe."[65]

Healing the Psyche

Because eating disorders involve the mind as well as the body, psychotherapy is a core component of treatment. Working with a therapist, teens learn to address the various factors that have contributed to the development of an eating disorder, as well as discover how to overcome negative thoughts and behaviors. The Mayo Clinic writes: "Individual psychotherapy can help you learn how to exchange unhealthy habits for healthy ones. You learn how to monitor your eating and your moods, develop problem-solving skills, and explore healthy ways to cope with stressful situations. Psychotherapy can also help improve your relationships and your mood."[66]

> Many studies have shown that family-based therapy can achieve dramatic results in helping eating disorder sufferers regain their health and recover.

It was therapy that finally helped Kandel learn how to start addressing the destructive thoughts that were at the heart of her eating disorder. "For the first time in my life," she writes, "I began to understand the feelings that underlay my eating disorder: why I hated myself so much, why I felt so undeserving, why I felt that everything had to be perfect."[67] This was both difficult and frightening for Kandel. She now knows that she could never have faced those painful thoughts if she had not come to the realization that she truly wanted to get better. She explains: "Up to that point, I honestly hadn't been willing. I just didn't want to. No one—including me—could love me enough for me to be encouraged to get better. I'd devoted ten years of my life to my eating disorder, and now, for the first time, I wanted to live, laugh and feel good about myself again."[68]

A Family Affair

Many studies have shown that family-based therapy (often called FBT) can achieve dramatic results in helping eating disorder sufferers regain their health and recover. Those who are most enthusiastic about this type of therapy maintain that when a teen suffers from an eating disorder, it is not his or her problem alone—the whole family is affected by it and should play a role in treatment. Daniel Le Grange, who is an associate professor of psychiatry at the University of Chicago Medical School and director of the school's Eating Disorders Program, explains the thinking behind family-based therapy: "In FBT, parents aren't blamed for their child's illness; instead, they're viewed as a crucial resource in bringing about their child's recovery."[69]

> As beneficial as treatment can be for teens with eating disorders, the sad reality is that most who suffer from them are never treated.

Family-based therapy involves three phases: weight restoration, or getting the teen back to a target weight as quickly as possible; teaching the teen to take control of eating; and helping him or her establish a healthy self-identity. In the first phase, it is up to parents to convince their teen that food for an eating disorder is like medicine for a disease, and he or she must eat—which can be excruciating for everyone involved. Someone who understands this well is Harriet Brown, a journalist who is the author of the book *Brave Girl Eating*. In using this method, Brown went through a terrible time with her teenage daughter, Kitty, who suffered from anorexia. After starving herself for so long, Kitty was petrified of starting to eat again. Brown writes: "The guilt my daughter Kitty felt about eating overpowered her own survival instinct, intellect, and hunger. When she defied the 'demon' inside her and ate, she suffered unbelievable anxiety, guilt, and terror."[70]

Brown and her husband were finally able to get Kitty to eat, but it took a great deal of hard work and dogged determination. When it was time for meals, they set aside a block of time and made sure that there were no interruptions, that nothing else happened until Kitty ate the food that was prepared and put in front of her. Brown writes: "I found that persistence and consistency were the keys. Sometimes I felt like a politician on-message, repeating one or two simple truths in a calm way: *I love you and I'm not going to let you starve. You need to eat all of this before you can go to school, take a shower, fill in the blank.*"[71] Once Kitty started eating again, she began to slowly regain the weight she had lost and was ready for the next phase of her treatment. Over time, because of the help from her parents and a team of dedicated professionals, she overcame her eating disorder.

Kitty Brown is a true success story among users of family-based therapy—and the method has helped numerous others recover as well. A study by Le Grange that was published in October 2010 involved 121 patients aged 12 to 18, most of whom were girls. All participants went through a year of either family-based therapy or individual therapy at the University of Chicago and Stanford University. At the end of 12 months, 49 percent of those who had been in family-based therapy were in full remission, compared with 23 percent who had been in individual therapy. Also, of the teens who were in remission, only 10 percent of the family-based therapy group had relapsed a year later, compared with a 40 percent relapse rate among the teens in individual therapy. Brown writes: "This finding marks the first time in 130 years of tracking the illness that we can identify a first-line treatment for teens with anorexia. And for millions of American families, that's the best news possible."[72]

When Teens Cannot Recover

As beneficial as treatment can be for teens with eating disorders, the sad reality is that most who suffer from them are never treated. According to the National Association of Anorexia Nervosa and Associated Disorders, only 10 percent of people with eating disorders receive treatment. There are various reasons for this, one of which is cost—which can be extraordinarily high and out of reach for many families. The Eating Disorders Coalition for Research, Policy & Action states that treatment for an eating disorder ranges from $500 to $2,000 per day in the United States.

Outpatient treatment, including therapy and medical monitoring, can run up a bill of more than $100,000. Even those who have health insurance are not always able to persuade their providers to pay for eating disorder treatment.

And then there are the teens who *do* receive treatment but still cannot overcome their eating disorders. This was the case with Frieda Curtis, a teenage girl from Wisconsin who struggled with bulimia for more than five years. To Curtis's family, it seemed like the girl wanted to get better. She often expressed her desperation in a journal, writing on one occasion: "I know I cannot throw up anymore because I know that's why my chest hurts and I don't want to die."[73] Curtis went through numerous treatment programs, including spending a week in a child and adolescent psychiatry program as a hospital inpatient, and a month-long outpatient program at a different hospital. She also met on a regular basis with an adolescent medicine specialist, as well as Scott Ritchie, a psychologist who specializes in eating disorders. Yet despite her desire to get better and the comprehensive treatment she went through, Curtis was unable to conquer her eating disorder. In November 2007 she died from a heart attack at the age of 19.

> " Once sufferers have conquered the demons that haunt them, they can begin to heal and move toward a brighter future. "

Ritchie was one of many who mourned Curtis's death, which was a tragic example of a teenager whose life was cut short by a devastating illness. "She was very aware of how serious it was," he says. "But she thought she could have control over it."[74] Ritchie says that in all of his 25 years of practice, Curtis was the first patient who died from an eating disorder during treatment.

There Is Hope

Eating disorders are serious and life threatening, and they can virtually take over someone's life. Yet even though treatment does not work for everyone, many teens can and do overcome these disorders. The recovery process involves a great deal of soul-searching, as well as the willingness to eat a healthy diet, to let go of obsessions with weight and body shape, and to work hard to rid oneself of destructive thoughts and behaviors. Once sufferers have conquered the demons that haunt them, they can begin to heal and move toward a brighter future. Kandel shares her thoughts:

> We all trip and fall along the way. But recovery is not about the trips and falls; it is about what happens after you pick yourself up. It's about getting back on your feet, dusting yourself off and moving forward, because that is how we learn. Realistically, neither life nor recovery is ever going to be a fairy tale, but we do have the power to create our own version of a real happily-ever-after.[75]

Primary Source Quotes*

Can Teenagers Overcome Eating Disorders?

66 **The prognosis of eating disorders in adolescents has varied widely in the literature. . . . Adolescent outcomes are significantly better than the outcomes reported in adults.** 99

> —David S. Rosen, "Clinical Report—Identification and Management of Eating Disorders in Children and Adolescents," *Pediatrics*, December 2010. http://pediatrics.aappublications.org.

Rosen is an eating disorder specialist who is a professor in the Department of Psychiatry at the University of Michigan Medical School.

66 **In my clinical experience, eating disorders tend to be extraordinarily tough to beat. . . . I've had several patients who were anorexic as teenagers, presumably fully recovered, who relapsed when their marriages broke up.** 99

> Cecilia M. Ford, "Eating Disorders: Not Just Kid Stuff Anymore," Women's Voices for Change, February 25, 2010. womensvoicesforchange.org.

Ford is a psychologist in private practice in New York City.

* Editor's Note: While the definition of a primary source can be narrowly or broadly defined, for the purposes of Compact Research, a primary source consists of: 1) results of original research presented by an organization or researcher; 2) eyewitness accounts of events, personal experience, or work experience; 3) first-person editorials offering pundits' opinions; 4) government officials presenting political plans and/or policies; 5) representatives of organizations presenting testimony or policy.

66 **Anorexia nervosa has a variable course and outcome. The course varies from spontaneous recovery without treatment to gradual or rapid deterioration, resulting in death.** 99

—S. Hossein Fatemi and Paula J. Clayton, eds., *The Medical Basis of Psychiatry*. Totowa, NJ: Humana, 2008.

Fatemi is a psychiatrist from Minneapolis, and Clayton is with the American Foundation for Suicide Prevention.

66 **Even after individuals have recovered from eating disorders, they are at risk of relapsing.** 99

—Andrea D. Vazzana, interviewed by Laurie Barclay, "Eating Disorders: An Expert Interview with Andrea D. Vazzana, Ph.D.," Medscape, March 6, 2009. www.medscape.com.

Vazzana is a clinical assistant professor of child and adolescent psychiatry at New York University.

66 **Because it's related to self-image—and not just about food—bulimia nervosa can be difficult to overcome.** 99

—Mayo Clinic, "Bulimia Nervosa," February 23, 2010. www.mayoclinic.com.

The Mayo Clinic is a world-renowned medical facility headquartered in Rochester, Minnesota.

66 **This is a treatable illness and over the last thirty years since I treated my first anorexic patient I have seen 90 percent of them recover and have a desk drawer filled with pictures of the children of my former anorexic patients.** 99

—Steven Levenkron, "Eating Disorders," Levenkron.com, 2010. www.levenkron.com.

Levenkron is a New York City psychotherapist who specializes in eating disorders and self-injury.

66 Unlike a problem with drugs or alcohol where part of the treatment is avoiding the substance altogether, people still have to eat. This can make it harder for someone with a binge eating problem to overcome it because the temptation to overeat is always there.99

—D'Arcy Lyness, "Binge Eating Disorder," KidsHealth, February 2009. http://kidshealth.org.

Lyness is a child and adolescent psychologist from Wayne, Pennsylvania.

66 Recovering to normal weight does not in and of itself signify a cure, because eating disorders are complex medical/psychiatric illnesses.99

—Alliance for Eating Disorders Awareness, "What Are Eating Disorders," 2010. www.allianceforeatingdisorders.com.

The Alliance for Eating Disorders Awareness seeks to educate the public about the dangers of eating disorders and reduce the rate and severity of these disorders among people of all ages.

Can Teenagers Overcome Eating Disorders?

- According to the National Association of Anorexia Nervosa and Associated Disorders, only **10 percent** of people with eating disorders receive treatment.

- According to the Eating Disorders Coalition for Research, Policy & Action, treatment for an eating disorder ranges from **$500 to $2,000 per day** in the United States.

- Outpatient treatment for eating disorders, including therapy and medical monitoring, can cost more than **$100,000**.

- According to the Eating Disorders Foundation of Victoria (Australia), **70 percent** of anorexia patients regain weight within 6 months of onset of treatment, and **15 to 25 percent** of them relapse, usually within 2 years.

- An April 2009 report by the Agency for Healthcare Research and Quality found that hospitalizations for eating disorders in children under age 12 jumped by **119 percent** between 1999 and 2006.

- According to the University of Maryland Medical Center, recovery from anorexia takes an average of **5 to 6 years** from the time of diagnosis.

Most Teens with Eating Disorders Are Not Treated

As beneficial as treatment can be for teens with eating disorders, research has shown that only about 1 out of 10 ever receives the help he or she needs. This was evident in a study published in January 2011 by National Institute of Mental Health researcher Kathleen Merikangas and her colleagues, who interviewed more than 10,000 youths aged 13 to 18. After determining that an average of 20 percent suffered from a serious mental disorder, the team tracked the rate at which the teens reported having ever received treatment specifically to treat their disorder.

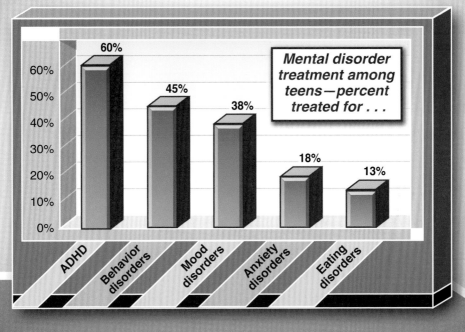

Mental disorder treatment among teens—percent treated for . . .

- ADHD: 60%
- Behavior disorders: 45%
- Mood disorders: 38%
- Anxiety disorders: 18%
- Eating disorders: 13%

Source: National Institute of Mental Health, "Majority of Youth with Mental Disorders May Not Be Receiving Sufficient Services," January 4, 2011. www.nimh.nih.gov.

- Studies have shown that **90 percent** of adolescent eating disorder sufferers treated with family-based therapy either recovered or made significant gains; five years after treatment, nearly **90 percent** were considered fully recovered.

Family-Based Therapy Has Best Results

Because eating disorders are as much about the mind as the body, psychotherapy is a crucial part of any treatment program. Research has shown that family-based therapy is more effective in treating teens with eating disorders than traditional one-on-one therapy. This was the focus of a study published in October 2010 that involved 121 anorexia patients aged 12 to 18. Each was randomly assigned to either one year of family-based therapy or one year of individual therapy, and the researchers found that the teens treated with family-based therapy had significantly better progress and lower relapse rates than the other group.

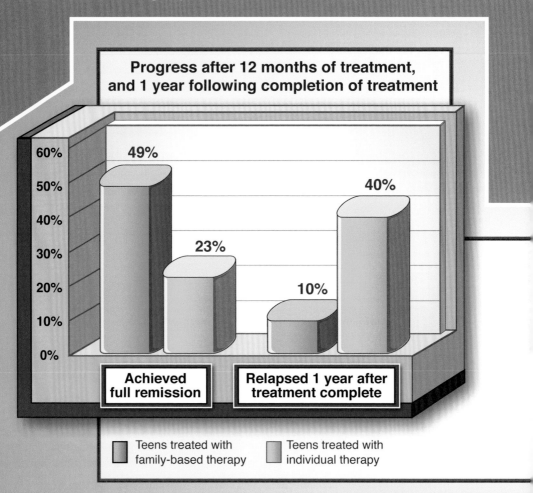

Progress after 12 months of treatment, and 1 year following completion of treatment

49%

40%

23%

10%

60%
50%
40%
30%
20%
10%
0%

Achieved full remission

Relapsed 1 year after treatment complete

Teens treated with family-based therapy

Teens treated with individual therapy

Source: James Lock et al., "Randomized Clinical Trial Comparing Family-Based Treatment with Adolescent-Focused Individual Therapy for Adolescents with Anorexia Nervosa," *Archives of General Psychiatry*, October 2010.

Low Federal Funding for Eating Disorder Research

Eating disorders collectively have the highest fatality rate of all mental illnesses, yet they receive a fraction of federal monies that are allocated for research into mental health disorders.

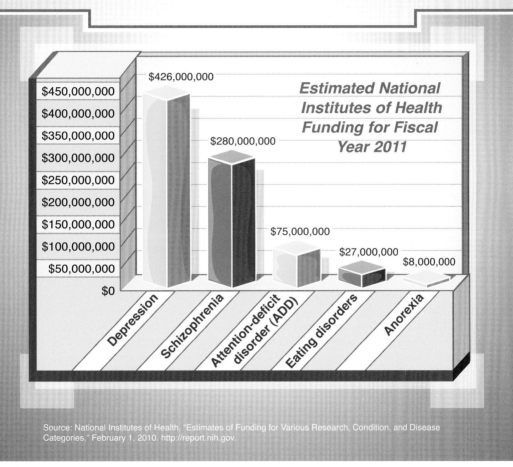

Estimated National Institutes of Health Funding for Fiscal Year 2011

- Depression: $426,000,000
- Schizophrenia: $280,000,000
- Attention-deficit disorder (ADD): $75,000,000
- Eating disorders: $27,000,000
- Anorexia: $8,000,000

Source: National Institutes of Health, "Estimates of Funding for Various Research, Condition, and Disease Categories," February 1, 2010. http://report.nih.gov.

- According to the National Eating Disorders Association, about **30 to 50 percent** of teens who have anorexia do not recovery by the time they reach their early- to mid-twenties.

Key People and Advocacy Groups

Academy for Eating Disorders: An organization that provides education and training for mental health professionals, as well as promotes research, treatment, and prevention for eating disorders.

Alliance for Eating Disorders Awareness: A group that educates young people about eating disorders and provides educational information to parents and health-care providers about the warning signs, dangers, and risks of eating disorders.

Hilde Bruch: A German-born psychoanalyst who in 1978 wrote *The Golden Cage: The Enigma of Anorexia Nervosa*, which is one of the first books ever written about the disease and is based on 70 of her patient cases.

Cynthia Bulik: A psychiatrist and renowned eating disorders specialist and researcher at the University of North Carolina–Chapel Hill School of Medicine.

Eating Disorders Coalition for Research, Policy & Action: An organization whose goal is to advance the recognition of eating disorders by promoting awareness among the public and policy makers and increasing resources for research, education, prevention, and improved training.

Walter H. Kaye: A psychiatrist and program director of the Eating Disorders Program at the University of California–San Diego.

Daniel Le Grange: An associate professor of psychiatry at the University of Chicago Medical School, the director of the school's Eating

Disorders Program, and the first to introduce the Maudsley Approach of family-based therapy in the United States.

Steven Levenkron: A well-known New York City psychotherapist who specializes in eating disorders and has written a number of books on anorexia, bulimia, and self-injury.

James Lock: A professor of psychiatry and behavioral sciences at Stanford University's School of Medicine and a recognized authority on eating disorders.

Vivian Hanson Meehan: A registered nurse from Highland Park, Illinois, who founded the National Association of Anorexia Nervosa and Associated Disorders in 1976.

National Association of Anorexia Nervosa and Associated Disorders: An organization that seeks to increase awareness of eating disorders and also serves as a resource center that provides information about eating disorders.

National Eating Disorders Association: A group whose goal is to expand public understanding and prevention of eating disorders, while promoting access to quality treatment and support for families through education, advocacy, and research.

David Rosen: A professor at the University of Michigan Medical School who is a well-known eating disorder specialist.

Chronology

1980
Anorexia nervosa is officially classified as a mental illness in the third edition of the American Psychiatric Association's *Diagnostic and Statistical Manual of Mental Disorders*; bulimia is considered only a symptom, not an independent disease.

1903
French psychologist Pierre Janet publishes a book called *Les Obsessions et la Psychasthénie*, in which he describes a patient named Nadia who engages in compulsive, secretive binge eating.

1966
Lesley Hornby, a 17-year-old girl from Britain who is known as "Twiggy," rises to international fame as a supermodel, and skinny, waiflike bodies become the norm in the fashion world.

1979
British psychiatrist Gerald Russell publishes a paper titled "Bulimia Nervosa: An Ominous Variant of Anorexia Nervosa," which is the first detailed written description of bulimia.

1900   **1960**   **1970**   **1980**

1873
In an address to the Clinical Society of London, physician Sir William Gull coins the term *anorexia nervosa* (meaning "nervous loss of appetite") to describe young girls who starve themselves in order to remain thin.

1976
The National Association of Anorexia Nervosa and Associated Disorders is founded in Highland Park, Illinois, and becomes the first organization in the United States devoted to eating disorders.

1978
Citing 70 case histories, German-born psychiatrist Hilde Bruch publishes one of the first books about anorexia, called *The Golden Cage: The Enigma of Anorexia Nervosa*.

1983
Singer Karen Carpenter dies of cardiac arrest as a complication of anorexia, and her death increases public awareness of the dangers of the disease.

1987
Bulimia nervosa is officially classified as a mental illness in the revised third edition of the American Psychiatric Association's *Diagnostic and Statistical Manual of Mental Disorders*.

2010
Two US senators from Minnesota and one from Iowa introduce the Federal Response to Eliminate Eating Disorders Act, which would direct the federal government to track, screen, diagnose, and treat eating disorders and improve access to treatment for eating disorder sufferers.

2009
A study by the Agency for Healthcare Research and Quality finds that eating disorder–related hospitalizations for children under the age of 12 increased 119 percent from 1999–2000 to 2005–2006.

1999
Through studies with patients who have recovered from anorexia, San Diego psychiatrist Walter Kaye discovers abnormally high levels of the brain chemical serotonin, an indication of differences in brain chemistry.

1990

2000

2010

1992
The term *binge-eating disorder* is officially introduced to describe people who binge eat but do not regularly use behaviors such as fasting or vomiting to lose weight.

2006
Based on studies with twins, researchers at the University of North Carolina–Chapel Hill and Sweden's Karolinska Institute conclude that 56 percent of the risk for developing anorexia is attributable to genetics.

2007
Eliana Ramos, an 18-year-old fashion model from Uruguay who suffered from anorexia, dies of a heart attack six months after her sister Luisel, also a model, died from the same cause. The deaths ignite widespread media attention over the self-starvation of models.

1994
Chicago psychiatrist Daniel Le Grange introduces the Maudsley Approach, a family-based therapy method of treatment for adolescents with eating disorders.

Related Organizations

Academy for Eating Disorders

111 Deer Lake Rd., Suite 100
Deerfield, IL 60015
phone: (847) 498-4274 • fax: (847) 480-9282
e-mail: info@aedweb.org • website: www.aedweb.org

The Academy for Eating Disorders is committed to being a leader in eating disorders research, education, treatment, and prevention. A good collection of articles and videos are available on its website, as well as a comprehensive eating disorders glossary.

Alliance for Eating Disorders Awareness

PO Box 13155
North Palm Beach, FL 33408-3155
phone: (866) 662-1235 • fax: (561) 841-0972
e-mail: info@eatingdisorderinfo.org
website: www.eatingdisorderinfo.org

The Alliance for Eating Disorders Awareness provides educational information to parents and caregivers about the warning signs, dangers, and consequences of eating disorders.

American Academy of Child & Adolescent Psychiatry (AACAP)

3615 Wisconsin Ave. NW
Washington, DC 20016-3007
phone: (202) 966-7300 • fax: (202) 966-2891
e-mail: info@aacap.org • website: www.aacap.org

The AACAP is a professional medical association whose 7,500 members actively research, evaluate, diagnose, and treat psychiatric disorders. Numerous articles about eating disorders can be accessed through the website's search engine, including a collection of fact sheets that are available in English and seven other languages.

Andrea's Voice Foundation

PO Box 2423
Napa, CA 94558
phone: (707) 224-8032
e-mail: doris@andreasvoice.org • website: www.andreasvoice.org

Founded by the mother of a teenage girl who died from complications of bulimia, this organization promotes an understanding of prevention, identification, diagnosis, and treatment of eating disorders. Its website offers a variety of downloadable materials about eating disorders.

Binge Eating Disorder Association

550M Ritchie Hwy. #271
Severna Park, MD 21146
phone: (443) 597-0066 • fax: (410) 741-3037
e-mail: info@bedaonline.com • website: www.bedaonline.com

The mission of the Binge Eating Disorder Association is to raise awareness, educate, and provide resources for its members and the general public. Its website offers an "About Eating Disorders" section, as well as research information, press releases, and current news.

Center for the Study of Anorexia and Bulimia

1841 Broadway, 4th Floor
New York, NY 10023
phone: (212) 333-3444 • fax: (212) 333-5444
e-mail: csab@icpnyc.org • website: http://csabnyc.org

The oldest nonprofit eating disorders clinic in New York City, the Center for the Study of Anorexia and Bulimia is devoted to treating individuals with eating disorders and training the professionals who work with them. Its website features an "Eating Disorders 101" section with information on all eating disorders, as well as links to many other resources.

Eating Disorders Coalition for Research, Policy & Action

720 Seventh St. NW, Suite 300
Washington, DC 20001
phone: (202) 543-9570
e-mail: manager@eatingdisorderscoalition.org
website: www.eatingdisorderscoalition.org

The mission of the Eating Disorders Coalition for Research, Policy & Action is to advance federal recognition of eating disorders as a public health priority. Its website offers articles about eating disorders, a synopsis of current research projects, information about federal policy, and a list of congressional briefings.

Families Empowered and Supporting Treatment of Eating Disorders (F.E.A.S.T.)

PO Box 331
Warrenton, VA 20188
phone: (540) 227-8518
e-mail: info@feast-ed.org • website: www.feast-ed.org

F.E.A.S.T. is an international organization whose goal is to help people recover from eating disorders by providing information and support, promoting evidence-based treatment, and advocating for research and education. Numerous articles are available on its website, along with video and audio presentations and an online forum.

National Association for Males with Eating Disorders, Inc.

118 Palm Dr. #11
Naples, FL 34112
phone: (239) 775-1145; toll-free: (877) 780-0080
e-mail: chris@namedinc.org • website: www.namedinc.org

With most resources focused on females, the National Association for Males with Eating Disorders seeks to fill that void by providing support to males suffering from eating disorders, along with educating the public and being an information resource. Its website provides statistics, articles about the various eating disorders, and information about prevention and treatment.

National Association of Anorexia Nervosa and Associated Disorders

PO Box 640
Naperville, IL 60566
phone: (630) 577-1333
e-mail: anadhelp@anad.org • website: www.anad.org

The National Association of Anorexia Nervosa and Associated Disorders seeks to prevent and alleviate the problems of eating disorders. Its website offers a quarterly newsletter, a number of informative fact sheets, a "Males & Eating Disorders" section, and news articles.

National Eating Disorder Information Centre

ES 7-421, 200 Elizabeth St.
Toronto, ON, Canada M5G 2C4
phone: (416) 340-4156; toll-free (866) 633-4220 • fax: (416) 340-4736
e-mail: nedic@uhn.on.ca • website: www.nedic.ca

The National Eating Disorder Information Centre provides information and resources on eating disorders, as well as food and weight preoccupation, and keeps the public informed about eating disorders and related issues. Its website offers a number of fact sheets, news articles, statistics, and cautionary information about pro-anorexia websites.

National Eating Disorders Association

603 Stewart St., Suite 803
Seattle, WA 98101
phone: (206) 382-3587 • fax: (206) 829-8501
e-mail: info@nationaleatingdisorders.org
website: www.nationaleatingdisorders.org

The National Eating Disorders Association works to prevent eating disorders and provides treatment referrals to those suffering from them. Found on its website are position statements, news releases, resources for eating disorder sufferers and families, and research papers.

National Institute of Mental Health (NIMH)

Science Writing, Press, and Dissemination Branch
6001 Executive Blvd., Room 8184, MSC 9663
Bethesda, MD 20892-9663
phone: (301) 443-4513; toll-free: (866) 615-6464 • fax: (301) 443-4279
e-mail: nimhinfo@nih.gov • website: www.nimh.nih.gov

An agency of the US government, the NIMH is the largest scientific organization in the world specializing in mental illness research and the promotion of mental health. Its website features statistics, archived *Science News* articles, and numerous publications accessible through its search engine.

For Further Research

Books

Stephanie Covington Armstrong, *Not All Black Girls Know How to Eat: A Story of Bulimia*. Chicago: Lawrence Hill, 2009.

Harriet Brown, *Brave Girl Eating: A Family's Struggle with Anorexia*. New York: William Morrow, 2010.

Lucy Howard-Taylor, *Biting Anorexia: A Firsthand Account of an Internal War*. Oakland, CA: New Harbinger, 2009.

Johanna S. Kandel, *Life Beyond Your Eating Disorder*. New York: Harlequin, 2010.

Gerri Freid Kramer, *The Truth About Eating Disorders*. New York: Facts On File, 2009.

Tammy Nelson, *What's Eating You? A Workbook for Teens with Anorexia, Bulimia, and Other Eating Disorders*. Oakland, CA: Instant Help/ New Harbinger, 2008.

Michele Siegel, Judith Brisman, and Margot Weinshel, *Surviving an Eating Disorder: Strategies for Family and Friends*. New York: Collins Living, 2009.

Carol Sonenklar, *Anorexia and Bulimia*. Minneapolis: Twenty-First Century, 2011.

Maria Stavrou, *Bulimics on Bulimia*. Philadelphia: Jessica Kingsley, 2009.

Periodicals

Suzanne Dooley-Hash, "I Will Never Fully Recover from Anorexia. That's Something I'm Reminded of Every Day," *Real Simple*, October 2010.

Karen Fanning, "Body Blow," *Scholastic Choices*, November/December 2010.

Marina Khidekel, "Can You Catch an Eating Disorder?" *Seventeen*, February 2010.

Meredith Matthews, "Just Can't Help It: People with Binge-Eating Disorder Feel Out of Control," *Current Health 2, a Weekly Reader Publication*, April/May 2009.

Kathleen McGuire, "Food Obsessed? The Dangerous Line Between Order and Disorder," *Dance*, October 2010.

Julie Mehta, "An Equal-Opportunity Destroyer: Meet Some Young Men Who Want You to Know the Truth About Eating Disorders," *Current Health 2, a Weekly Reader Publication*, February 2010.

New Moon Girls, "The Truth About Size: Boost Your Body Confidence," May/June 2010.

Jane Shin Park, "Thin Ice," *Teen Vogue*, September 2009.

Abigail Pesta, "Fighting with Food," *Marie Claire*, May 2009.

Jessica Press, "The ED [Eating Disorder] Diaries," *Seventeen*, March 2009.

Christine Richmond, "What Eating Disorders Do to Your Body," *Glamour*, March 2010.

Internet Sources

Harriet Brown, "She's Not That Skinny. Is She?" *Psychology Today*, August 13, 2010. www.psychologytoday.com/blog/brave-girl-eating/201008/shes-not-skinny-is-she.

Hilary Fey Cronin, "Skewed Notions of Beauty Can Kill," *Wisconsin State Journal*, November 22, 2008. http://host.madison.com/news/opinion/article_defca536-c07d-5dee-a454-a50ea1ab9b97.html.

Mayo Clinic, "Eating Disorders," January 15, 2010. www.mayoclinic.com/health/eating-disorders/DS00294.

Camille McConnell, "Low Self Esteem: Fueling the Eating Disorder," *Basil & Spice*, May 2, 2010. www.basilandspice.com/mind-and-body/52010low-self-esteem-fueling-the-eating-disorder.html.

National Association of Anorexia Nervosa and Associated Disorders, "About Eating Disorders," 2010. www.anad.org/get-information/about-eating-disorders.

Source Notes

Overview

1. Quoted in Sean Keeler, "How Did Anorexia Take Krista Phelps?" *Des Moines Register*, August 2, 2010. http://m.dmregister.com.
2. Quoted in Keeler, "How Did Anorexia Take Krista Phelps?"
3. National Institute of Mental Health, *Eating Disorders*, 2008. www.nimh.nih.gov.
4. Alexander R. Lucas, *Demystifying Anorexia Nervosa*. New York: Oxford University Press, 2008, p. 91.
5. Quoted in Caring Online, "Males and Eating Disorders," 2010. www.caringonline.com.
6. National Eating Disorders Association, "Common Myths About Eating Disorders," 2008. www.nationaleatingdisorders.org.
7. Kimberly Dennis, "What Is Bulimia?" DailyStrength, December 30, 2009. www.dailystrength.org.
8. Mayo Clinic, "Eating Disorders," January 15, 2010. www.mayoclinic.com.
9. Quoted in Tiffany Chan, "False Reflection: MU Professor Studies How, Why Eating Disorders Consume Females in U.S.," *Missourian*, February 6, 2009. www.columbiamissourian.com.
10. Kathleen N. Franco, "Eating Disorders," Cleveland Clinic, August 1, 2010. www.clevelandclinicmeded.com.
11. Quoted in David Ninh, "Model Ali Michael's Struggle with Eating Disorders and Her Career," *Dallas Morning News*, June 16, 2008. www.dallasnews.com.
12. Rosalind Ponomarenko-Jones, "Why Pictures of Scarily Skinny Celebrities Should Carry a Health Warning, by a Mother Whose Daughter Died of Anorexia," *Daily Mail*, April 5, 2010. www.dailymail.co.uk.
13. Ponomarenko-Jones, "Why Pictures of Scarily Skinny Celebrities Should Carry a Health Warning, by a Mother Whose Daughter Died of Anorexia."
14. National Eating Disorders Association, "Common Myths About Eating Disorders."
15. Sharon Farber, interviewed by David Roberts, "Getting Help for Self-Harm," HealthyPlace, April 11, 2007. www.healthyplace.com.
16. Lucas, *Demystifying Anorexia Nervosa*, p. 83.
17. National Association of Anorexia Nervosa and Associated Disorders, "About Eating Disorders," 2010. www.anad.org.
18. Michael Levine, interviewed by Judith Banker, "Q & A with Michael Levine, Ph.D.," Center for Eating Disorders at Sheppard Pratt, April 14, 2009. http://eatingdisorder.org.
19. Quoted in Amanda Gardner, "Eating Disorders, Addictions Tough to Treat in Teens," *U.S. News & World Report*, July 1, 2010. http://health.usnews.com.
20. Quoted in MedlinePlus, "Anorexic Teens May Gain from Whole-Family Treatment," October 4, 2010. www.nlm.nih.gov.

What Are Eating Disorders?

21. Quoted in Cynthia Busuttil, "Claudia Faniello Speaks About the Monster That Ruled Her Life," *Times of Malta*, March 18, 2009. www.timesofmalta.com.
22. Quoted in Busuttil, "Claudia Faniello Speaks About the Monster That Ruled Her Life."

23. Quoted in Busuttil, "Claudia Faniello Speaks About the Monster That Ruled Her Life."

24. Susan Schulherr, *Eating Disorders for Dummies*. Hoboken, NJ: Wiley, 2008, p. 11.

25. Schulherr, *Eating Disorders for Dummies*, p. 10.

26. Hilde Bruch, M.D., *The Golden Cage: The Enigma of Anorexia Nervosa*. Cambridge, MA: Harvard University Press, 1978, p. vii.

27. Julie O'Toole, "Eating Disorders Are Biological Illnesses of the Brain," blog, Kartini Clinic for Disordered Eating, April 27, 2010. www.kartiniclinic.com.

28. Alliance for Eating Disorders Awareness, "Did You Know?" 2011. www.allianceforeatingdisorders.com.

29. Jessica Bennett, "It's Not Just White Girls," *Newsweek*, September 6, 2008. www.newsweek.com.

30. Quoted in Katrina Tupper, "Psychology Behind an Eating Disorder," *State Hornet*, January 18, 2010. www.statehornet.com.

31. Johanna S. Kandel, *Life Beyond Your Eating Disorder*. New York: Harlequin, 2010, p. 15.

32. Andrea D. Vazzana, interviewed by Laurie Barclay, "Eating Disorders: An Expert Interview with Andrea D. Vazzana, Ph.D.," Medscape, March 6, 2009. www.medscape.com.

33. Anna Paterson, *Beating Eating Disorders Step by Step*. London: Jessica Kingsley, 2008, p. 23.

34. Laura Peachey, "Bulimarexia Support," Facebook, 2009. www.facebook.com.

35. Steven Bratman, "What Is Orthorexia?" Orthorexia Home Page, June 4, 2010. www.orthorexia.com.

36. Steven Bratman, "Fatal Orthorexia," Orthorexia Home Page, June 3, 2010. www.orthorexia.com.

37. Quoted in Busuttil, "Claudia Faniello Speaks About the Monster That Ruled Her Life."

Why Do Teenagers Develop Eating Disorders?

38. Ovidio Bermudez, "Eating Disorders: Much Progress but Still Far to Go," *Psychiatric Times*, May 1, 2008. www.psychiatrictimes.com.

39. James Lock, e-mail interview with author, January 4, 2011.

40. Quoted in Michigan State University, "MSU Researchers Discover Potential Genetic Factor in Eating Disorders," news release, June 4, 2010. http://research.msu.edu.

41. O'Toole, "Eating Disorders Are Biological Illnesses of the Brain."

42. Quoted in Denis Campbell, "Anorexia Risk 'Could Be Predicted,'" *Guardian*, March 29, 2009. www.guardian.co.uk.

43. Quoted in Denis Campbell, "Anorexia Risk 'Could Be Predicted.'"

44. Mayo Clinic, "Eating Disorders."

45. Paterson, *Beating Eating Disorders Step by Step*, p. 9.

46. Paterson, *Beating Eating Disorders Step by Step*, p. 9.

47. Paterson, *Beating Eating Disorders Step by Step*, p. 10.

48. Paterson, *Beating Eating Disorders Step by Step*, p. 10.

49. Aimee Liu, *Gaining: The Truth About Life After Eating Disorders*. New York: Warner, 2007, p. 41.

50. Allison Kreiger Walsh, "Profile in Recovery: Allison's Story," in *Life Beyond Your Eating Disorder*, by Johanna S. Kandel. New York: Harlequin, 2010, p. 32.

51. Walsh, "Profile in Recovery," p. 32.

What Are the Dangers of Eating Disorders?

52. Quoted in Liz Hull, "Girl, 15, Who

Went on a Post-Christmas Diet Dies from Anorexia in a Year," *Daily Mail*, September 29, 2010. www.dailymail. co.uk.

53. Quoted in Hull, "Girl, 15, Who Went on a Post-Christmas Diet Dies from Anorexia in a Year."

54. Schulherr, *Eating Disorders for Dummies*, p. 78.

55. Schulherr, *Eating Disorders for Dummies*, p. 79.

56. Quoted in Gina Shaw, "Anorexia: The Body Neglected," WebMD, November 8, 2007. www.webmd.com.

57. Marcia Herrin and Nancy Matsumoto, *The Parent's Guide to Eating Disorders*. Carlsbad, CA: Gürze, 2007, p. 117.

58. Quoted in Shaw, "Anorexia."

59. Herrin and Matsumoto, *The Parent's Guide to Eating Disorders*, p. 116.

60. Ruchi Mathur, "Diabulimia—Eating Disorder," MedicineNet, February 22, 2008. www.medicinenet.com.

61. Mathur, "Diabulimia—Eating Disorder."

62. Paterson, *Beating Eating Disorders Step by Step*, p. 212.

Can Teenagers Overcome Eating Disorders?

63. Johanna Kandel, interviewed by Loren's World, "The Truth About Eating Disorders," November 22, 2010. www.lorensworld.com.

64. Kandel, *Life Beyond Your Eating Disorder*, p. 25.

65. Quoted in HealthyPlace, "Eating Disorders: Anorexia Nervosa—the Most Deadly Mental Illness," January 10, 2009. www.healthyplace.com.

66. Mayo Clinic, "Eating Disorders."

67. Kandel, *Life Beyond Your Eating Disorder*, p. 25.

68. Kandel, *Life Beyond Your Eating Disorder*, p. 25.

69. Daniel Le Grange, foreword to Harriet Brown, *Brave Girl Eating*. New York: HarperCollins, 2010, p. xi.

70. Harriet Brown, "Going Through Hell? Keep Going," *Psychology Today*, September 11, 2010. www.psychology today.com.

71. Harriet Brown, "Getting My Daughter to Eat," *Psychology Today*, August 26, 2010. www.psychologytoday.com.

72. Harriet Brown, "Hope for Teens with Anorexia," *Psychology Today*, October 13, 2010. www.psychologytoday.com.

73. Quoted in David Wahlberg, "How Bulimia Killed Frieda 'This Was a Girl Who Thought She Was Fat and Ugly,'" *Wisconsin State Journal*, November 16, 2008. http://host.madison.com.

74. Quoted in Wahlberg, "How Bulimia Killed Frieda 'This Was a Girl Who Thought She Was Fat and Ugly.'"

75. Kandel, *Life Beyond Your Eating Disorder*, p. 3.

List of Illustrations

Index

Note: Boldface page numbers indicate illustrations.

About the Author

Peggy J. Parks holds a bachelor of science degree from Aquinas College in Grand Rapids, Michigan, where she graduated magna cum laude. An author who has written over 100 educational books for children and young adults, Parks lives in Muskegon, Michigan, a town that she says inspires her writing because of its location on the shores of Lake Michigan.